Strategic Management - a Dynamic View

Edited by Okechukwu Lawrence Emeagwali

Published in London, United Kingdom

IntechOpen

Supporting open minds since 2005

Strategic Management - a Dynamic View
http://dx.doi.org/10.5772/intechopen.77102
Edited by Okechukwu Lawrence Emeagwali

Assistant to tje Editor(s) Hassan Yousef AlJuhmani

Contributors
Dandy George Dampson, Alexander Kyei Edwards, Charles McMillan, Tsitsi Mufudza, Yung Yau, Daniel Chi Wing Ho, Rowedah Hussien, Hafeth Naji, Ehsan Kareem, Okechukwu Lawrence Emeagwali, Hasan Yousef Aljuhmani

First published in London, United Kingdom, 2019 by IntechOpen
IntechOpen is the global imprint of INTECHOPEN LIMITED, registered in England and Wales, registration number: 11086078, 7th floor, 10 Lower Thames Street, London, EC3R 6AF, United Kingdom
Printed in Croatia

British Library Cataloguing-in-Publication Data
A catalogue record for this book is available from the British Library

Additional hard and PDF copies can be obtained from orders@intechopen.com

Strategic Management - a Dynamic View
Edited by Okechukwu Lawrence Emeagwali
p. cm.
Print ISBN 978-1-83962-504-6
Online ISBN 978-1-83962-505-3
eBook (PDF) ISBN 978-1-83962-506-0

For EU product safety concerns:
IN TECH d.o.o., Prolaz Marije Krucifikse Kozulić 3, 51000 Rijeka, Croatia, info@intechopen.com or visit our website at intechopen.com.

Meet the editor

Dr. Okechukwu Lawrence Emeagwali holds a PhD in Management (Strategy Focus) from Girne American University, Cyprus, where he is currently an associate professor of strategic management and Head of the Department of Business Management. Dr. Emeagwali is also the Director of the faculty's Center for Management Research, and the current President of the American Academic Research Society, USA. He is a member of the Strategic Management Society and actively researches within the field of strategic management. His current research interests focus on understanding the strategic and disruptive thinking patterns among upper echelons and top management teams. Dr. Emeagwali has authored and coauthored over 20 publications in internationally refereed journals. His fields of interest include strategic management, strategic thinking, disruptive strategies, competitive and cooperative strategies, upper echelons, top management teams, corporate governance, and corporate social responsibility.

Contents

Preface

Decades after predicting an increase in the intensity of competition levels—usually occurring gradually or quickly depending on the nature of industry—scholars such as Josef Schumpeter and Richard D'Aveni have not only been vindicated, but the competitive dynamics stream of strategic management research is a direct product of decades of research on the dynamics of competition they inspired. These studies have been conducted specifically in industries such as the automobile, airline, and retail industries experiencing these increases in levels of competition—the so-called hypercompetitive industries.

While extant literature contains a sizable number of review papers on strategy research à la competitive dynamics, there have not been sufficient aggregation or collections of non-competition-based studies of dynamism in hypercompetitive industries. This edited book is strategically poised to explore other aspects of strategy dynamism, not just those restricted to competition.

Readers will find the six constituent chapters informative and insightful from diverse industry and geographic perspectives.

Dr. Okechukwu Lawrence Emeagwali
Associate Professor of Strategic Management,
Head, Department of Business Management,
Director, Center for Management Research,
Girne American University,
Cyprus

Section 1

Introduction

Chapter 1

Introductory Chapter: Strategic Management - A Dynamic Approach

Okechukwu Lawrence Emeagwali
and Hasan Yousef Aljuhamni

1. Introduction

Schumpter [1] and D'Aveni [2] persistently declared that industries irrespective of their nature, (static or dynamic) are experiencing and will continue to experience increasing levels of competition. Decades later evidence abounds in support of their postulations [3–13]. Latching on to this realization that irrespective of the traditional nature of industries, advances in technology are spurring increasing levels of industry competition, a lot of scholars have examined the antecedents of succeeding in this era for both organizations competing in traditionally turbulent or hypercompetitive industries as well as for organizations operating in traditionally static industries.

A review of extant literature reveals that some key antecedents for succeeding in the face of increasing levels of industry competition irrespective of industry nature include the development and use of dynamic strategies, dynamic leadership and dynamic capabilities-including organizational learning capabilities through transactive memory systems and general knowledge management as well as dynamism in strategic decision making [14–30].

The purpose of this edited volume is to sensitize readers on the state of current research on the role of dynamism in the strategy discourse.

2. On dynamic strategies

A vast body of current literature inextricably linking dynamism to success in traditionally dynamic and hypercompetitive markets exists in literature. This volume contains chapters which provide support to the continuous relevance of dynamism in this regard. This body of literature collectively examines the continuous relevance of the recommendation that dynamic strategy, capabilities and competences are pivotal for success in turbulent and hypercompetitive markets. Its collective findings signify that conscious choices regarding the deployment of dynamic strategies made by top management determine differentials in dynamic capabilities and competences observable among competing firms in hypercompetitive industries, and this in turn, determine the adaptability and flexibility differentials observable among such firms—a necessary and existential condition for survival and succeeding in such industries.

While the above findings naturally apply to organizations competing in highly competitive industries and markets, a second body of literature also represented

IntechOpen

in this volume reveals that the same can be said of organizations which operate in traditionally static or stable markets. In particular, this second but related body of literature found links between dynamic strategy approaches and organizational performance in traditionally static environments in line with the early postulations about the increasing levels of competitive rivalries currently being experienced by all types of industries by Schumpeter [1] and D'Aveni [2] as well as other prominent competitive dynamics scholars [10, 17, 31–37].

Interestingly, while this finding implies that even organizations competing in traditionally static industries such as higher education need to develop dynamic capabilities, latest research within this sub-domain also points to the fact that even static industries operating in the least competitive regions of the world such as Africa also need to become nimble and dynamic to stay ahead in their industries.

In other words, readers will come to the conclusion after reading this volume, that irrespective of the nature of an industry or the economic region within which it is situated, there is need for the development and deployment of advanced strategic thinking competences at the corporate governance level in a bid to develop unique dynamic strategies, capabilities and competencies which then confer upon organizations the strategic flexibility for increased adaptability to rapidly increasing changes in otherwise static industries such as the higher education industry [32, 33, 36, 37].

3. On dynamic capabilities

Diving deeper to the firm level of analysis, this volume also lends itself to studying individual capabilities and competencies which contribute to the strategic agility necessary for survival and succeeding in increasingly hypercompetitive markets, further contributing to the dynamic capabilities literature by providing a diverse perspective particularly emanating from the context of emerging and developing economies.

Readers should expect to find contributions to the theoretical underpinnings of the dynamic capabilities' literature such as agency and stewardship theories among others; as well as a reiteration of the importance of other non-tangible capabilities such as corporate identity and reputation during strategy development and competitive interactions. Most importantly, readers would find empirical evidence that newer capabilities emanating from exponential technologies such as artificial intelligence are increasingly changing the dynamic capabilities landscape introducing novel capabilities that engender speed and flexibility within firms and dictate new competitive rules within industries, irrespective of type.

4. Conclusions

All in all, the mission of this edited volume is to present current empirical evidence for the continued relevance of dynamism in the strategy discourse. It finds that dynamism in the development and execution of strategies and its dependence on dynamic capabilities is still very relevant in today's business environment, irrespective of whether these environments are hypercompetitive in nature or relatively stable. It also finds that irrespective of whether firms operate in highly competitive geographic regions or less competitive ones—typically characteristic of most developing economies, strategic dynamism is of equal importance and relevance.

The findings of this volume is important and significant because the randomness with which the constituent chapters were selected and the diverse nature of the study backgrounds involved, give credence to the role that dynamism continues to play within the field of strategic management.

Author details

Okechukwu Lawrence Emeagwali* and Hasan Yousef Aljuhamni
Faculty of Business and Economics/Center for Management Research,
Girne American University, Kyrenia, Cyprus (Northern)

*Address all correspondence to: lawrenceemeagwali@gau.edu.tr

References

[1] Schumpeter J. Capitalism, Socialism and Democracy. 3rd ed. New York, NY: Harper; 1950

[2] D'Aveni RA. Waking up to the new era of hypercompetition. The Washington Quarterly. 1998;**21**(1): 183-195

[3] Baum JAC, Korn HJ. Competitive dynamics of interfirm rivalry. Academy of Management Stable. 2019;**39**(2):255-291

[4] Chen M, Miller D. Competitive attack, retaliation and performance: An expectancy-valence framework. Competitive Attack, Retaliation and Strategic Management Journal. 1994;**15**(2):85-102

[5] Emeagwali OL, Çalicioğlu C. Competitive interaction: Nature, volume and patterns of generic competitive actions executed by the three largest mobile telecommunication network operators in Turkey. Problems and Perspectives in Management. 2014;**12**(1):181-190

[6] Chen M, Miller D. Reconceptualizing competitive dynamics. The Academy of Management Annals. 2012;**6**(434):1-83

[7] Turgay T, Emeagwali OL. Hypercompetition: The driving force behind successful business innovations? A critical review of literature. Investment Management and Financial Innovations. 2012;**9**(3):111-119

[8] Ferrier WJ. Navigating the competitive landscape: The drivers and consequences of competitive aggressiveness. The Academy of Management Journal. 2001;**44**(4):858-877

[9] Jacobson R. The "Austrian" School of Strategy. Academy of Management Review. 1992;**17**(4): 782-807. Available from: https://www.jstor.org/stable/258808

[10] Mohammad Alzoubi A, Lawrence Emeagwali O. Do generic strategies impact performance in higher educational institutions? A SEM-based investigation. Business and Economic Horizons. 2017;**12**(2):42-52

[11] Emeagwali OL, Çalıcıoğlu C. Industry-specific competitive actions within the Turkish mobile telecommunications network operating industry. International Journal of Business and Social Sciences. 2014;**5**(5)

[12] Young G, Smith KG, Grimm CM, Science SO, Issue S, Young G, et al. "Austrian" and industrial organization perspectives on firm-level competitive activity and performance. Organization Science. 1996;**7**(3):243-254

[13] Emeagwali OL, Çalicioğlu C. Mapping the generic competitive action types peculiar to the Turkish mobile telecommunications network operating industry. Problems and Perspectives in Management. 2014;**12**(1):51-59

[14] Bradshaw R, Chebbi M, Oztel H. Leadership and knowledge sharing. Asian Journal of Business Research. 2015;**4**(3):1-20

[15] Carmeli A, Atwater L, Levi A. How leadership enhances employees' knowledge sharing: The intervening roles of relational and organizational identification. The Journal of Technology Transfer. 2011;**36**(3):257-274

[16] Emeagwali OL. In: Emeagwali OL, editor. Corporate Governance and Strategic Decision Making [Internet]. Rijeka: IntechOpen; 2017. Available from: https://www.intechopen.com/books/corporate-governance-and-strategic-decision-making

[17] Elrehail H, Emeagwali OL, Alsaad A, Alzghoul A. The impact of Transformational and Authentic leadership on innovation in higher education: The contingent role of knowledge sharing. Telematics and Informatics [Internet]. 2018;**35**(1): 55-67. Available from: https://doi.org/10.1016/j.tele.2017.09.018

[18] Alzghoul A, Elrehail H, Emeagwali OL, AlShboul MK. Knowledge management, workplace climate, creativity and performance: The role of authentic leadership. Journal of Workplace Learning. 2018;**30**(8):592-612

[19] Alshanty AM, Emeagwali OL, Ibrahim B, Alrwashdeh M. The effect of market-sensing capability on knowledge creation process and innovation evidence from SMEs in Jordan. Management Science Letters. 2019;**9**:727-736

[20] Alshanty AM, Emeagwali OL. Market-sensing capability, knowledge creation and innovation: The moderating role of entrepreneurial-orientation. Journal of Innovation & Knowledge [Internet]. 2019. DOI: 10.1016/j.jik.2019.02.002

[21] Al-Tal MJY, Emeagwali OL. Knowledge-based HR practices and innovation in SMEs. The Organ. 2019;**52**(1):6-21

[22] Alatailat M, Elrehail H, Emeagwali OL. High performance work practices, organizational performance and strategic thinking: A moderation perspective. International Journal of Organizational Analysis. 2019

[23] Gumusluoglu L, Ilsev A. Transformational leadership, creativity, and organizational innovation. Journal of Business Research. 2009;**62**(4):461-473. DOI: 10.1016/j.jbusres.2007.07.032

[24] Hmieleski KM, Cole MS, Baron RA. Shared authentic leadership and new venture performance. Journal of Management. 2012;**38**(5):1476-1499

[25] RS-J L. The relationships between transformational leadership, knowledge sharing, trust and organizational citizenship behavior. International Journal of Innovation, Management and Technology. 2014;**5**(3):3-6

[26] Lin HF. Knowledge sharing and firm innovation capability: An empirical study. International Journal of Manpower. 2007;**28**(3-4):315-332

[27] Reiter-Palmon R, Illies JJ. Leadership and creativity: Understanding leadership from a creative problem-solving perspective. The Leadership Quarterly. 2004;**15**(1):55-77

[28] López B, Monfort A. Creating shared value in the context of sustainability: The communication strategy of MNCs. In: Emeagwali OL, editor. Corporate Governance and Strategic Decision Making. 2017. pp. 119-135

[29] Aykan E. Gaining a competitive advantage through green human resource management. In: Emeagwali OL, editor. Corporate Governance and Strategic Decision Making. 2017

[30] Wang GY. Taking corporate social responsibility as growth strategy. In: Emeagwali OL, editor. Corporate Governance and Strategic Decision Making. 2017. pp. 105-117

[31] Jarrar Y, Emeagwali L, Awobamise A. Attracting younger millennials: Lifting bond out of a transitional sinkhole. Dirasat: Human and Social Sciences. 2019;**46**(1):115-123

[32] Resnick DP. Innovative universities: When, why and how? International Journal of Educational Planning & Administration. 2012;**XXVI**(2):331-341

[33] Silver H. Managing to innovate in higher education. British Journal of Educational Studies. 1999;**47**(2):145-156

[34] Brown R. Higher education and the market. Journal of Higher Education. 2011;(2014):1-231

[35] Emeagwali OL, Naghdipour B. Exploring the usage and user-perception of interactive white boards in higher education in North Cyprus. The Procedia—Social and Behavioral Sciences. 2013;**83**:272-276. DOI: 10.1016/j.sbspro.2013.06.053

[36] Gaspar D, Mabic M. Creativity in higher education. Universal Journal of Educational Research. 2015;**3**(9):598-605

[37] Brennan J, Ryan S, Ranga M, Broek S, Durazzi N, Kamphuis B. Study on innovation in higher education: Final report. In: Originally available from European Commission Directorate for Education and Training Study on Innovation in Higher Education [Internet]. 2014. Available from: http://eprints.lse.ac.uk/55819/1/__lse.ac.uk_storage_LIBRARY_Secondary_libfile_shared_repository_Content_Durazzi%2CN_Studyinnovation_Durazzi_Studyinnovation_2014.pdf

Section 2

On Dynamic Strategies

Chapter 2

Dynamic Strategy in a Turbulent Business Environment

Tsitsi Mufudza

Abstract

Today's turbulent business environment, characterised by rapid technological changes and increased globalisation, has swept away industry and market conditions that previously defined competitive conditions. Such an environment requires flexible strategic solutions that respond quickly to these rapid changes. This chapter will therefore look at the need for dynamic strategy in today's business basing on the systematic review of relevant literature. It will also focus on the need for dynamic capabilities and competencies that are necessary for coping with the ever changing business environment. The chapter highlights that capability differentials among firms are a result of choices made by management. This explains why some firms are more adaptive than others and more flexible firms have been seen to perform better under uncertain environments.

Keywords: strategy, dynamic strategy, turbulent business environment, dynamic capabilities, dynamic competencies

1. Introduction

This chapter discusses the need for a dynamic strategy in turbulent business environment. The chapter starts by giving definitions to key terms like strategy and turbulent business environment. Tools that have been traditionally used to cope with environmental uncertainty have been looked at and how they can be complemented to yield better strategies and improve performance in a turbulent business environment.

2. Methodology

In this chapter the methodology employed was the qualitative systematic review of literature on the various aspects of the topic addressed which include strategy, dynamic strategy, turbulent business environment and dynamic capabilities among others. Basic ideas on how to conduct such a systematic review were borrowed from prominent scholars in the area [1]. Both integrative and interpretative techniques were used to uncover new understanding in the area of strategy. Using this methodology, various studies on dynamic strategy and turbulent business environment were brought together from various primary qualitative studies conducted and some in depth study on the subject matter was done resulting in conclusions being drawn. Thus qualitative synthesis of literature review was used as a basis for the arguments discussed in this chapter.

3. Strategy

Strategy can be described as a plan of action that is designed to achieve a particular goal. Thus strategy is concerned with the setting and achieving of objectives and the process also involves the allocation of resources, which requires some consistency and cohesiveness of actions and decisions [2]. From its conception as a discipline, soon after the second world war, strategy has been greatly associated with systematic and detailed planning which distinguished it from other forms of planning. However this conception has been greatly challenged in the past few years as the business environment has become more dynamic and turbulent. Some strategic tools to cope with uncertainty in a turbulent business environment have been rendered ineffective, hence the need to seriously consider the phenomenon of strategy in a turbulent business environment. Thus there has been great emphasis on the need to shift from regarding strategy as a detailed and systematic plan to considering them as mere guidelines for action in a dynamic business environment. However research has proven that strategy is an indispensable aspect even in a turbulent environment though there is need to move away from traditional approaches to strategy and embrace more reactive approaches centred on strategic agility and organisational flexibility.

4. Turbulent business environment

Turbulence can be best described as 'unpredictable uncertainty for strategic planning purposes' [3]. Environmental uncertainty is believed to arise when managers are not 'confident that they understand the major changes and events in their industries' [4]. Such an environment has also been regarded by some scholars as 'hypercompetitive' and it was taken to refer to 'an environment of fierce competition leading to unsustainable advantage or the decline in the sustainability of advantage' [5]. Earlier work on turbulence can be traced back to the work on capitalism and creative destruction [6]. However a hypercompetitive environment is regarded as surpassing the earlier 'creative destruction' of the 1930s which was mainly as a result of technological innovation and revolution [5]. Environmental turbulence can be taken to have been necessitated by several aspects which include rapid product innovation, changes in customer tastes and preferences, increased rates of technology transfer, employee and talent mobility, new internet capabilities, rapid technological changes and globalisation. Earlier studies attributed such changes to aspects like the emergence of trading blocks, excess capacity, structural changes, environmental concerns, reduced protectionism and technological discontinuities among others [7]. Failure to anticipate and embrace changes brought by these forces has been greatly attributed to the changing fortunes of the former leading and largest companies like General Motors, IBM and Xerox [7].

Thus, research has shown that a turbulent business environment defies the key assumptions of traditional strategic planning which are regarded as mostly applicable in identifiable and stable industry structures [5, 7, 8]. This therefore necessitated the re-evaluation of most strategic management tools and concepts. For instance, sustainable competitive advantage, which was regarded as a key component of a good strategy, was regarded as non-existent and instead organisational flexibility and dynamic capabilities were considered as sources of sustainable advantage [5, 8]. Furthermore, arguments around Porter's Five Forces model and the Resource Based View (RBV) of the firm were challenged since they were taken to be based on a stable business environment. This was due to the difficulties associated with measuring and assessing buyer, supplier and rivalry power as industries' boundaries become blurred and hard to define in turbulent environments. Under such conditions the major underlying assumptions of the RBV were also defied as factor markets were considered as moving towards constant disruption and perfection as a result of rivalry and innovation.

Thus under hypercompetitive conditions, temporary rather than sustainable advantages have been identified as existing and new theories like 'entrepreneurial action' [9] were formulated to replace some traditional strategic models. Changes in the business environment can either be incremental (also termed evolutionary or continuous) or discontinuous (revolutionary). Under these types of change different strategic approaches are called for to enable firms to cope with the growing uncertainty.

5. Tools for coping with environmental uncertainty

Various tools have been traditionally used by firms to cope with strategic planning in fast paced business environments. These tools include environmental scanning, scenario analysis, real options analysis and technology and product road mapping. These tools and techniques have been used to identify drivers of change in the external business environment of companies. These tools will be looked at below, but it should not go unmentioned that these tools have been criticised on the grounds that most drivers of change interact in ways that are novel and unforeseeable to be easily detected by these tools.

5.1 Environmental scanning

Environmental scanning has been regarded as a process of acquiring and using information about trends, events and relationships in an organisation's external environment which assists management in planning the future course of action [10]. It is believed that environmental scanning is well defined, systematically planned and executed and that it is directed at systematic and comprehensive data. This process is also taken to rely on regular, casual and informal information sources from all stakeholders [11] and it involves both information searching and viewing [10]. Organisations carry out environmental scanning so that they understand the external forces at work and develop effective responses to improve or secure their position in the future. They also scan the environment in order to identify opportunities and threats, avoid surprises, gain competitive advantage and enhance their short and long term planning.

The ability of an organisation to adapt to its external environment depends heavily on its knowledge and interpretation of external changes at work. The quality of the information gathered from the scanning process or of the environmental scanning process itself is determined by the cognitive abilities of management. Furthermore, the organisation's ability to survive depends on its ability to align its internal activities with the external constituents. Thus the scanning process should provide good quality (anticipatory) information that enables it to respond to the future developments in the environment by creating innovative entrepreneurial behaviour [11].

Research has shown a positive correlation between environmental scanning and improved organisational performance [10]. However scanning alone has been regarded as insufficient to assure performance, but it should be aligned with strategy and the information obtained must be effectively utilised in the strategic planning process. It has been recommended that scanning should enhance and increase discussion and communication about future oriented planning in organisations and should induce strategic and organisational learning.

5.2 Scenario analysis

Scenario analysis is one technique used to measure operational risk in organisations. Operational risk is defined as 'the risk of loss resulting from inadequate or failed internal processes, people or systems or from external events' [12]. Scenario analysis is a quantitative tool used to assess the impact of extreme events based on hypothesis or historical scenarios. It can be identified as a stress testing tool that allows institutions to obtain useful results from examining scenarios that cover infrequent but selective risks that can have a great impact on institutional operations.

In scenario analysis estimations are based on 'what-if' scenarios that are generated on the basis of catastrophic events that occurred in other organisations, external data, expert opinion or extremely imagined events [11]. It is meant to investigate whether an organisation would be able to undergo exceptional risk losses. Basically there are two groups of scenarios whose classification is determined by the event type they define. The first category makes use of historical events like the September 2011 terrorist attacks or a strike and management investigates the potential impact of these events on the organisation. The second group uses hypothetical scenarios like some plausible risk events that have not yet happened but have some probability to occur.

However great care must be taken in using scenario analysis since it is very subjective and depends heavily on the choice of the scenarios used. Thus the use of irrelevant scenarios or bad assumptions can result in irrelevant losses.

5.3 Real options analysis

A real option is regarded as the 'right but not the obligation to acquire, expand, contract, abandon or switch some or all of an economic asset on fixed terms on or before the time the opportunity ceases to be available' [13]. As suggested in the definition, some examples of real options include:

- Option to switch resources
- Option to expand
- Option to delay
- Option to wait and see
- Option for future growth

Real options use options theory to evaluate physical or real assets and they give certain reactive plasticity on decision makers like the options to divest, wait or invest in in the face of new information. Traditionally, real options have been used to analyse troubled firms and firms involved in research and development with considerable amounts managerial flexibility under significant amounts of uncertainty.

The real options approach is highly regarded since it ponders upon numerous decision pathways in the face of high uncertainty. It also gives management room for flexibility in selecting the optimal strategies or options along the way when new information becomes available. This approach is credited for assuming a multidimensionality series of decisions that give management room to adapt in the face of changes in the business environment. This helps management to hedge themselves against negative risks. Thus management has room to make strategy adjustments in the case of future uncertainty. Furthermore, as information becomes available and uncertainty clears, management can choose the best strategies to implement.

5.4 Technology and product road mapping

This is a technology forecasting tool that aims at improving the 'strategic technology planning process by linking the acquisition of technology to strategic objectives and the associated business and market drivers, enabling soundly-based technology investment to be taken' [14]. Technology and product road mapping is used by companies to determine the future technological evolutions and appropriate actions that would enable companies to compete and survive in such a future.

It is believed that technology road mapping has gone through two generations and that a third generation stage is still at its infantry stage [14]. The first generation is believed to have emerged from the 1970s to the mid-1980s. This generation is believed to have been centred on methodologies aimed at forecasting technology more accurately and clearly. The second generation was centred on methodologies aimed at improving strategic technology planning decisions and it span from the mid-1980s to the end of 1990s. The third generation with methodologies aimed at producing integrated technology management activities is believed to have emerged from the end of the 1990s to date. However it is believed that very few companies have adopted the third generation due to lack of supporting software that enable them to integrate it into their business processes.

6. Strategic foresight

The above tools have been commonly used by businesses to enhance decision making at business and corporate level strategies. Since most of the techniques are future oriented, the terms 'strategic foresight' and 'corporate foresight' have been used to encompass these practices [4]. Strategic foresight is defined as a 'future-intelligence gathering and medium to long-term vision-building process that aids present day decisions and mobilises joint actions in a systematic and participatory way' [4].

It is also defined as a set of technologies, tools, methods and actions that are used to provide an accurate description of both the present-day and future business environment of an entity [15]. It is considered as combining both expert analysis and technology to determine the most influential factors in the business environment that will have considerable effect on business development. Strategic foresight is also considered to happen 'when any planner uses scanned inputs, forecasts, alternative future exploration analysis and feedback to produce or alter plans and actions of the organization' [16].

Strategic foresight has been criticised due to its failure to make reliable predictions [4]. It is argued that although the predictions of strategic foresight are relatively accurate in the short run, forecasting accuracy is likely to diminish in the medium and long run due to the unpredictability nature of technological, economic, political and social drivers of change that work together in unusual and unanticipated ways. Therefore, reactive methodologies based on strategic agility and organisational flexibility have been encouraged under turbulent environments instead of planning.

However research has shown that there are certain circumstances under which foresight based approaches and planning are useful in helping the alignment of strategic decisions with changing environments. Furthermore, there are also circumstances under which flexible approaches are useful. For instance, in a study conducted on strategic planning and organisational flexibility in turbulent environments, it was found that in the case of continuous drivers of change that do not result in boundary uncertainty, strategic foresight tools are useful. Organisations operating under such circumstances are therefore encouraged to invest heavily in predicting changes and new events and align them with their goals. However the same study above also found that in the case of discontinuous change, which results in boundary uncertainty, managers should emphasise agility and stay flexible so that they adapt to environmental changes as they develop. The study also found that in the case of discontinuous change, foresight techniques and practices like product and technology road mapping can become sources of indolence which may lock managers 'into the (wrong) future they predicted and thus distracting them from the real future' [4].

The above was the case of Nokia which was locked in its Symbian operating systems that it had invested so heavily in. Nokia had used environmental scanning, product and technology roadmaps to define its competitive position and developing its product portfolio in the mobile communication industry. However, Nokia was not able to sustain its advantage over Google and Apple which entered the market unexpectedly exploiting the software skills they had originally developed in the PC industry. This entry of Apple and Google into the market can be identified as an example of a discontinuous driver of change that results in boundary uncertainty. Thus under such circumstances, strategic flexibility and learning enable firms to grasp the new key components and players of their industry as soon as they emerge and adapt quickly.

The above brings us to the issue of dynamic strategy which contends that strategic planning is dynamic and it involves a complex pattern for actions and reactions. Thus strategy making can thus be planned and partially unplanned.

7. Dynamic capabilities

A capability is defined as a 'collection of organizational routines that enable a firm to perform some set of tasks on a repeated or consistent basis' [17]. Capabilities are taken to encompass 'organisational processes by which resources are utilised to create growth and adaptation within changing environments' [18]. Capability identification, selection and creation is an important (practical) strategic decision whose competitive performance is equivalent to decisions about 'which markets to enter, how a firm can position itself in the market, in which markets to exploit existing resource capabilities, what prices to charge, how to deter entry and other traditional strategic variables' [19]. Thus in the same manner business organisations compete in markets for products, they also compete to create technological, operational and organisational capabilities that provide them with advantage in those product markets. This entails a positive correlation between decision about product market entry and position and decision capability creation [19].

It has been argued that investments in capabilities create strategic options for competition in product markets, and the firm's capability strategy is to make a choice of investments in different types of capabilities. From a capabilities perspective, the firm's strategic problem has been regarded as that to choose among alternative investment paths for building capabilities that would underlie competitive advantage [20]. The formation of capabilities is a result of various kinds of activities that include autonomous learning by doing, business process redesign, experimentation, investments in human and physical capital, technology adoption and Research and Development projects [19].

It has been posited that the firm's capability strategy involves choosing between deepening their existing capabilities contrasted with broadening their capabilities collection to include new sets of capabilities and this has been demonstrated in the form of a map with some examples provided [19]. This map is shown in **Figure 1**.

The above author argued that companies' investments in capabilities can either be specialised or generalised as indicated in the map. However it was posited that both specialised and generalised capabilities can be subjected to broadening and deepening investments. For example as shown in **Figure 1**, when Honda (well known for automobile production) engages in vehicle design simulation methods, this is a typical capabilities' deepening investment. However when Honda engages in building capabilities in light jet design, this is a typical capabilities broadening investment.

Likewise Google's expansion into auto designs is an example of broadening investment, whereas Google's research and development on internet search is an example of deepening investment as shown in **Figure 1**.

Dynamic has been defined as the 'capacity to renew competences so as to achieve congruence with the changing business environment' [21]. Thus dynamic capabilities are taken to represent the 'firm's ability to integrate, build and reconfigure internal and external competences to address rapidly changing environments' [21].

As explained earlier on, the essence of dynamic capabilities emerged after the realisation through research that sustainable advantages suggested by traditional strategy theories are rare, short-lived and may be fortuitous [7]. As a result, dynamic capabilities and organisational capabilities were regarded as sources of sustainable competitive advantage. However it should be pointed out that there has been no empirical evidence established to the effect of the sustainability of capabilities over extended periods, though it has been established that inertia and complacency weaken the sustainability of dynamic capabilities [7].

The dynamic capabilities theory is regarded as an extension to the Resource Based View (RBV) framework which argues that competitive advantage is a result of the firm's ability to manage its internal resources. This is because some resources are regarded as firm specific, not transferrable and difficult to imitate. Thus in the RBV framework, a firm is regarded as a 'collection of resources that are valuable, rare, imperfectly imitable and non-substitutable' [22]. However, the RBV has been criticised on the grounds that while it identifies mechanisms that build competitive advantage, it does not explain how these mechanisms operate [22].

Dynamic capabilities are a framework that is used to understand differences in firm level capabilities. The framework holds that firm level differences in

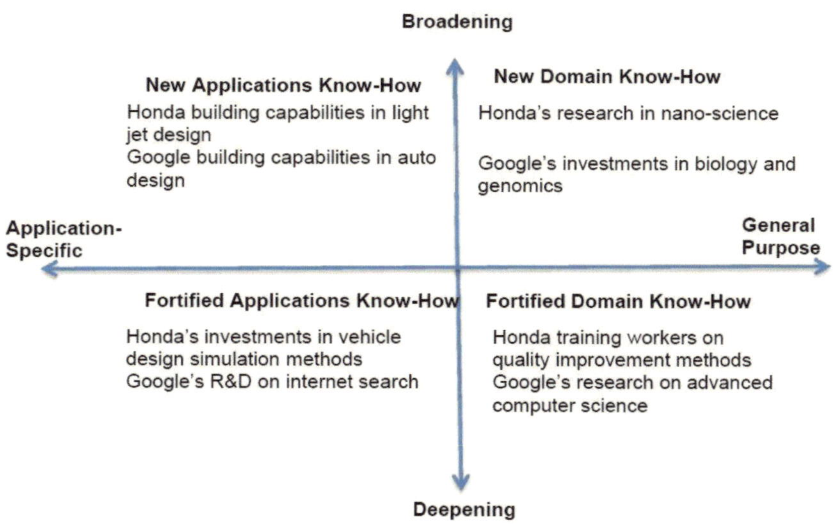

Figure 1.
Map for capability strategy choices. Source: Pisano [19].

capabilities are rooted in three factors namely asset positions, processes and paths which are explained below.

a. Asset positions—which hold that a firm's ability to change the future range of capabilities is constrained by its current stock of capabilities. Here assets refer to the legacy resources namely organisational competences, technical skills and knowledge that determine the firm's options for future capability expansion.

b. Processes—which refer to aspects like management systems, resource allocation processes and governance structures that shape organisational adaptability. It is this capacity to reconfigure a firm's asset positions and specifically the processes that underlie this capacity that led to the formation of the construct called dynamic capabilities.

c. Paths—which hold that since most capabilities develop over time and are cumulative in nature, they involve commitments to 'paths' instead of discrete projects. This entails firms to engage themselves in paths for capability that lead to competitive advantage.

It is believed that capability differentials across firms is mainly a result of management choices, and management must be able to influence the creation and evolution of their firms' capabilities. Thus management discretion in the selection of paths, together with some constraints faced can result in differences in firm capabilities. The dynamic capabilities approach can be used to explain firm level differentials and it also assists managers in making capability decisions. The approach helps to explain why some firms are more adaptive than others. More flexible firms are likely to do better in uncertain environments.

8. Conclusion

In conclusion, it can be posited that, in a dynamic business environment, traditional tools for copying with strategic planning are necessary but not sufficient in ensuring business sustainability. Furthermore the nature of changes experienced determine the strategic approaches adopted by managers. Managers should also make proper capabilities decisions that will enable their firms to cope with uncertainty experienced in their business environments.

Author details

Tsitsi Mufudza
Chinhoyi University of Technology, Chinhoyi, Zimbabwe

*Address all correspondence to: tsimufudza@gmail.com

References

[1] Gülmezoglu AM, Chandler J, Shepperd S, Pantoja T. Reviews of qualitative evidence: A new milestone for Cochrane. Cochrane Database of Systematic Reviews. 2013;(11):1-2

[2] Grant RM. Contemporary Strategy Analysis: Text and Cases Edition. New Jersey: John Wiley & Sons; 2016

[3] Ramírez R, Selsky JW. Strategic planning in turbulent environments: A social ecology approach to scenarios. Long Range Planning. 2016;**49**(1):90-102

[4] Vecchiato R. Strategic planning and organizational flexibility in turbulent environments. Foresight. 2015;**17**(3):257-273

[5] D'Aveni R. Hypercompetition: Managing the Dynamics of Strategic Management. Free Press: New York; 1994

[6] Schumpeter JA. Change and the Entrepreneur. Essays of JA Schumpeter; 1934

[7] Prahalad CK, Hamel G. Strategy as a field of study: Why search for a new paradigm? Strategic Management Journal. 1994;**15**(S2):5-16

[8] D'Aveni RA, Dagnino GB, Smith KG. The age of temporary advantage. Strategic Management Journal. 2010;**31**(13):1371-1385

[9] Smith KG, Cao Q. An entrepreneurial perspective on the firm-environment relationship. Strategic Entrepreneurship Journal. 2007;**1**(3-4):329-344

[10] Choo CW. Environmental scanning as information seeking and organizational knowing, vol. 1. Prima Vera Working Paper. 2002

[11] Rupcic N, Zekan SB. Business environment scanning: Prerequisite for sustainable learning company. In: An Enterprise Odyssey. International Conference Proceedings. University of Zagreb, Faculty of Economics and Business; 2012, June. p. 1132

[12] Rippel M, Teply P. Operational risk-scenario analysis. World Academy of Science, Engineering and Technology, International Journal of Social, Behavioral, Educational, Economic, Business and Industrial Engineering. 2010;**4**(6):723-730

[13] Robinson I, Kyng T. Real Options Analysis: The Challenge and the Opportunity. Institute of Actuaries of Australia Biennial Convention; 2003

[14] Gindy NN, Cerit B, Hodgson A. Technology roadmapping for the next generation manufacturing enterprise. Journal of Manufacturing Technology Management. 2006;**17**(4):404-416

[15] Strategic Foresight White Paper. 2013. www.agentielle.com

[16] Coates J, Durance P, Godet M. Strategic foresight issue: Introduction. Technological Forecasting and Social Change. 2010;**77**(9):1423-1425

[17] Winter SG. Understanding dynamic capabilities. Strategic Management Journal. 2003;**24**(10): 991-995

[18] Pettus ML, Kor YY, Mahoney JT. A theory of change in turbulent environments: The sequencing of dynamic capabilities following industry deregulation. International Journal of Strategic Change Management. 2009;**1**(3):186-211

[19] Pisano GP. A Normative Theory of Dynamic Capabilities: Connecting Strategy, Know-How, and Competition. 2015

[20] Teece D, Pisano G. The dynamic capabilities of firms: An introduction. Industrial and Corporate Change. 1994;**3**(3):537-556

[21] Teece DJ, Pisano G, Shuen A. Dynamic capabilities and strategic management. Strategic Management Journal. 1997;**18**(7):509-533

[22] El Gizawi N. The dynamic capabilities theory: Assessment and evaluation as a contributing theory for supply chain management [bachelor's thesis]. University of Twente; 2014

Chapter 3

Strategic Thinking, Leadership and Governance for African Universities: Lessons from Successful Universities

Dandy George Dampson and Alexander Kyei Edwards

Abstract

In the 21st century, global competition is forcing tertiary institutions to excel in knowledge-creation that are relevant and innovative to bring solutions to societal problems. Perhaps a new system of thinking will enhance the relevance and sustainability of these universities. The paper takes a look at successful African universities and the lesson that can be learned from them. In depth discussions regards strategic thinking, leadership and governance of African universities are well digested with views and expectations collected through interviews with both past and current universities leadership. Majority of the views and expectations were drawn from successful universities in Ghana.

Keywords: African universities, governance, leadership, strategic thinking

1. Introduction

The ability to think strategically is essential for individuals and institutions. The real question is how can we continually be more focused on our strategic thinking skills in order to thrive in today's unstable higher education management? The fact is most higher education leaders in Africa are now required to be more successful with fewer resources [1]. In 2009, several authors commissioned by the Association of African Universities (AAU) pointed out that Higher Education Institutions (HEI) are struggling with strategic thinking, re-thinking, and sustainability issues and that HEIs may need to improvise on their knowledge creation ventures [2–4]. In Africa, specifically in Ghana, higher educational (universities) leaders have limited resources to varying degrees within their educational institutions. The reality, however, is that not all higher educational leaders are good strategists.

In these current times, global competition is forcing tertiary institutions to excel in knowledge-creation that are relevant and innovative to bring solutions to societal problems. Perhaps a new system of thinking will enhance the relevance and sustainability of African universities. In Ghana for example, PNDC Law provides technical leadership, entrepreneurial solutions, and support for industries for national development.

At the global frontier of knowledge-creation is the need for change forced by internal and external factors, competition, demand and supply of tertiary education. Institutions of higher learning are advised to examine institutionalized systems, in order to innovate for the twenty-first century (C21st) emerging market and the global competition by thinking strategically [5, 6]. Strategic thinking is different from strategic planning that most institutions are noted for [7]. Strategic thinking is the construct of "ideas, processes and tools; of finding new and innovative approaches to problem solving and using policy initiatives and approaches that allow for effective implementation, monitoring and refining" [5], which strategic planning is not [7].

Evidence from research across the globe affirms that strategic thinking is more crucial at the time when in Ghana's tertiary education landscape is changing. Since 1992 there has been a policy and a gradual implementation of recommendations from the Ministry of Education Technical Committee report [8] on the conversion of Ghana Polytechnics to Technical Universities (TUs). As expected such policies are subjected to scrutiny and critique; many are wondering how ready are the Polytechnics to assume TUs and how successful is this policy for national development. Fortunately, the Ghana government and National Council for Tertiary Education (NCTE) have decided to start with five Polytechnics. However, the success of such a policy have a tremendous impact on tertiary education in the country and hence, a matter of concern for stakeholders. The implementation of the policy document [8] outlined strategies and plausible changes that will facilitate the growth of these institutions that are mandated to provide:

- Tertiary education in the fields of manufacturing, commerce, science, technology, applied social science, applied arts and any other fields approved by the Ministry of Education

- Opportunity for skills development, applied research and publication of research findings [8].

A review of the policy objectives shows that there are likely challenges in the policy implementation. There is the need for strategic planning, strategic management, a dyadic relation between ideals and actual performances, and the need to bring expected results in the policies and implementation framework [8].

This chapter will take an in-depth look at Strategic Thinking, Leadership and Governance for African Universities: Lessons from Successful Universities with special reference to Ghana, and Lessons learned from successful universities.

2. Strategic thinking: the concept

The concept of strategic thinking has been debated by scholars and practitioners for the last 25 years in an effort to understand its meaning and impact on organizational leadership and performance. Although the concept is gaining interest, it is still an area considered to be under-researched [9] as there is a lack of supporting empirical literature to clarify the role of strategic thinking in leadership effectiveness [10, 11]. This has resulted in a lack of theoretical understanding, leaving little guidance for leaders [10]. Fairholm and Fairholm [12] conceptualize strategic thinking competency as a work in progress in the world of academic literature. The mere lack of a common definition for strategic thinking has led to the concept being considered indecisive [13, 14] and even being confused and interchangeably used with other leadership and management concepts such as strategy, strategic planning and strategic management [9, 13, 15]. Mintzberg [16] states that 'many practitioners and theorists have wrongly assumed that strategic planning, strategic thinking, and strategy-making are all synonymous'. However, recent studies have refined the existing literature on strategic thinking, thereby distinguishing it from the other strategy types [17–19]. This reworking of the definition of strategic thinking is triggered by the popularity of and attention to this concept as being critical to leadership effectiveness [19]. Similarly, the uncertainty, complexity and turbulence of the contemporary world of business have demanded that organizational leaders and managers think strategically in order to ensure survival of their businesses [15, 18].

What is known in literature as strategic thinking is different from strategic planning or strategic management, particularly when it comes to organizational or institutional advancement [5, 7, 20]. In Africa and other developing countries literature is silent when it comes to strategic thinking and that of higher institutional advancement. According to [20], strategic thinking is a creative endeavor fused with "dynamic, responsive, and often intuitive" (p. 456) influence on an enterprising goal. In strategic thinking, the inputs, throughouts, and outputs are expected to feed into what to change in a system to ensure efficiency within a *SMART* goal [7] – where a SMART goal means Specific, Measurable, Aligned, Realistic and Time-bound.

Edwards and Sam [6] made an attempt to encourage a *Feedback* in strategic thinking loop, whether positive or negative, whereby its effects are cumulative in an appreciative enquiry. They urge that strategic thinking in higher institutions must be guided by the *"Brain Powers"* of the institution. It is perceived that their collective *"Brain Power"* in strategic thinking will impact results if solicited systematically and efficiently. What is missing in most African literature is how institutions can encourage "the engagement of people in such a way that leaders and followers raise one another to higher levels of motivation and morality" [21], through the process of strategic thinking for institutional change [6]. In effect, faculty and staffs need to contribute and own the ideas, and to provide inputs into the processes of change.

A study conducted by [1] found that strategic leadership influences activities and the thinking behind ideas in order to 'move people' to accomplish change. For example; one the institutional leader's echoed through interview that to lead strategically, *"Institutional leaders must lead academically ... and in solving social problems ... leave those politicians ... [if] they [politicians] create problems, ... We [academicians] must be there to solve them". "Our institutional leadership's commitment [is to] be solving societal problems rather than talking and lamenting with the rest of the society .... People need solutions from our research and academic activities" (DDG, Interviewee #1).* Strategic leadership when it comes to policy implementation is all about moving people with minimal efforts and maximum resources to accomplish expected goals [7, 22]. Leadership becomes strategic with much thinking about relations and tasks, not just directing, especially in higher education, but ownership to the processes [23]. Strategic leadership is a vehicle for controlling systems, planned changes, and moving people to buy-into ideas, following willingly, and sharing a common vision [7, 23].

Therefore when it comes to a whole system change in a tertiary institution in Ghana, for example, there is a gap in literature on the application of leader-follow interactions. But it is significant for the dynamic interchange of "thinking" and "influencing". First of all, every vision must be shared, communicated, and spread with a passion that becomes contagious [22]. It was evident in their study [1] that institutional leadership in African universities has to think of ways to demonstrate passion and commitment to a dream for others to believe and yield to any systematic change. Whereby strategic change can only take place when people are ready and looking forward to a better alternative [24]. According to the [24], when it comes to strategic change, leadership plays a vital role: systems will remain, individuals are comfortable, and groups will come to inertia, if leadership does not focus on the alternative change. Where leadership is not content with traditions they provide alternatives and "strategic management methodologies can be a stimulant to strategic thinking" [5] devoid of rituals and "sacred" traditions that inhibit creativity and innovations.

2.1 Entrepreneurship and scholarship

Entrepreneurship is based on the premises of providing solutions to human problems. In an attempt to define entrepreneurship based on reviews, [25] identify *"two distinct clusters of thought on the meaning of entrepreneurship. The first ... characteristics of entrepreneurship (e.g., innovation, growth, uniqueness, etc.) while the second group focused on the outcomes of entrepreneurship (e.g., creation of value)* (p. 12). This means entrepreneurship is viewed as both characteristics and resultants. In each case, according to [25], entrepreneurship involves innovations, peculiar to creating value for new products and services, and the "creation of organizations" that result in employability (self or otherwise). However, this definition falls short of mentioning the object of entrepreneurship, which should always result in solving social or human problems [26]. Baumol [27] however, believes that entrepreneurship is more significant when it is conceived as productivity than activities. Baumol [27] contests that private enterprise is more towards profit and not necessarily innovations (*that to him is not entrepreneurship*). He argues against the conventional understanding of entrepreneurial roles when it comes to growing the economy. Rather to [27] some entrepreneurship leads to "parasitical existence that is actually damaging to the economy" (p. 894). Therefore the notion is that strategic thinking about entrepreneurship should lead to a social enterprise, especially socioeconomic development policies in Africa [28].

For strategic thinking in entrepreneurship, [26] establishes 10 rules. These 10 rules are practical, productive, and evident. They include full commitment, a search for solutions, creative thinking, acting with others (teams), acting alone (uniqueness), managing risks, learning to lead, and selling ideas (marketing), perseverance, and above all, a passion to "play the game for life". This is where strategic thinking enhances entrepreneurship to solve socioeconomic problems with dedication and commitment. According to [26] thinking, entrepreneurship has to bring about value-added and an improvement for the good of the society. Entrepreneurship without a sense of socio-moral obligation, a "*Preference for Others*" to reach attainable success can possibly lead to what is prevalent in the modern business world – *Greed* [26]. Perhaps it is this sense of socio-moral obligation, accountability, societal benefits, leads itself to a scholarship of engagement to the public good.

Scholarship is the ability to produce knowledge that can stand any academic scrutiny and general attention [29-31]. Here scholarship connotes a personal or a group attention to the creation of sound knowledge which are original and transferable. According to [29], scholarship aside from knowledge creation allows vigorous interrogation. In academia scholarship is a significant way to bring new ideas, inventions, creativity, and originality by encouraging academic attainment [30]. Scholarship is therefore evident in research, experiments, and investigations that advance theories, professional abilities, and life skills. Scholarships methodologically lead to professional acumen, aptitude, and behavioral change resulting from and through learning. These sentiments were captured in an interview with institutional leaders in Burkina Faso;

> *One could see the pride of belongingness and institutional scholarship of engagement as:*

"[We] the PSI community felt a moral commitment to engage in academic research ... that brings dedication and commitment to solving Burkina problems" (Interviewee #1).

He continued:

"Our research has to focus on bringing social relevance which has also resulted in inventions, techniques, ... and we are socio-culturally responsible for conservation and innovations as higher education community".

Burkina Faso has a climate that result in acute water shortage, dry seasons and sanitary problems especially in the capital Ouagadougou where the case study institute is situated.

"So, see, at PSI we specialized". "Academic excellence will come when you specialize in what you can do best"(Interviewee #1) [1].

Thus, entrepreneurship augments scholarship, which intends leads to improved lifestyle, solutions for life problems, innovations through critical thinking, and socio-moral development, all of which culminate professionalism among citizens. Professionalism becomes more of an individual development that is associated with meaningfulness in human capital and socio moral obligation to the diversity of a given society [31]. Edwards [31] opines that professionalism brings a sense of belongingness, institutionalization of moral reasoning that usually impact on the provision of tangible solutions for the good of 'others' without a sense of discrimination [31, 32]. However literature is yet to establish significant association between moral development and scholarship of engagement in a wide perspective when it comes to benefits to society. The few research available show a nexus between moral obligation, individual self-development, and that of institutional accomplishments [32]. In other words, there is a demand for literature to show how institutions of higher learning may exert much more influence on society based on their relevant acquisition of knowledge, skills and abilities, contribute to scholarship of engagement for strategic development (Scholarship of Engagement, n.d., para. *Introduction*).

This is a normative conception that resonate socio-moral responsibility of public and statutorily established institutions. This is because society expects such institutions to give back for the socio-economic development. But when the society overlooks such normative conception scholarship is affected, application of scholarship in terms of relevance is deluded, and the attraction of scholarship in the society becomes illusive (Scholarship of Engagement, n.d). The concept of *Scholarship of Engagement* is a term that captures scholarship in the areas of teaching, research, and/or service ... [that] engages faculty in academically relevant [solution to] ... community needs" (para. *Introduction*).

2.1.1 Technology and learning

In today's tertiary education in Ghana, due to the challenge of geographical and diverse constituents, management cannot afford to lack behind in knowledge and skills in information and communication technology. Firstly, for strategic thinking management needs information fast and evidence for decision making. Finding information at a click is just request appropriate for speedy decision. Managers and leadership of higher education have to rely on new learning technologies for communicative and collaborative efforts and to facilitate 'real time' learn. The ICT for virtuality (remote communication), authentication, and e-leadership are all available for accelerating communication, certification, and governance decisions. For example; the distance education unit in the University of Education, Winneba, has instituted a new department for e-learning to all distance education student to facilitate teaching and learning. Similarly, all students are made to offer a compulsory course in ICT. There is no doubt that researchers argue that technology can be used to develop formal thinking through stimulation. However, technology-based stimulation will not automatically develop the thinking skills of leaders unless careful thought and planning are put in place to implement them effectively.

Secondly, for teaching and learning, which is the core business of every higher education, the role of technology is prominent in instructional leadership, resources mobilization and provision, and therefore the institutionalization of technology-mediated instructional delivery is for efficiency and effectiveness. Also, for roper governance in the C21st education system there is the need to embark on digitization of contents, repository of knowledge, and electronic archiving of contents, history, and proceedings. Tertiary institutions rely mostly on evidence from the statutes, rules, regulations, and precedence. So apart from the physical and telecommunication infrastructural challenges, the intersection between e-leadership and e-learning are yet to be advanced in practice by many institutions. But for strategic planning, new learning technologies within the framework of proper management and governance have to focus on results-driven efficiency through high competencies in technology.

2.2 Strategic implementation: perspectives from African universities

In their search for sustainable advantage, researchers have realized that business performance is not concentrated on the formulation alone but also on the implementation of a given strategy and further strengthened by the processes by which competitive positions are created and maintained [33]. For [34], strategic implementation is the method by which strategies are operationalized or executed within the organization. It focuses on the processes through which strategies are achieved. Once the means and methods for achieving objectives and mission have been identified, the next step according to [35] is to begin "doing". This stage involves the continuation of some ongoing strategies as well as the beginning of some new strategies [36]. As a result, managers should consider analysis of organizational structures and systems before strategy implementation, as well as the analysis of culture, power and conflict [37]. To effectively implement and manage the strategy, managers must integrate the activities of several different functions. These activities help to achieve the best integration of people, structures, processes and resources in reaching organizational purposes.

In regard to strategic implementation, Universities such as University of Ghana, Legon, Kwame Nkrumah University of Science and Technology, University of Education, Winneba, University of Cape Coast, Cape Town University in South Africa and other universities in Africa employ numerous strategic implementations such as research, teaching and learning, gender and diversity and monitoring and evaluation.

2.3 Research strategies

The core mandate of every university is to teach and research. Therefore, it argued among researchers that teaching cannot be productive with effective research. If this argument holds, then the implication is that for university to be successful, research should be at the hob of its operations [38]. In this regard research is centralized to the every University's transformation process, and ultimately strengthening their impact and visibility both locally and internationally. A study conducted by [1, 6] shared some common features of research strategies adopted by successful universities in Ghana and Burkina Faso. Most successful universities in Africa implemented their research strategies through:

- Collaboration with local and international institutions as well as donor agencies.
- Establishing and joining global research networks.
- Establishing competitive research studentships.
- Building capacity in craftsmanship, apprenticeship and entrepreneurship.

In creating a greater focus on inter-disciplinary research, successful universities in Africa adopted the following measures:

1. Acquiring state-of-the-art equipment and improve facilities (including library access) as a necessary foundation for academic research.
2. Developing and implementing a plan for increasing the pool of University controlled funds available for academic research.
3. Establishing University-Industry partnerships to promote research in areas of industrial/national interest.
4. Developing and implementing training and career development programs for staff involved in research and research support.
5. Providing stronger institutional support across the university in the administration and development of research grants.
6. Provide stronger institutional support across the university in the administration and development of research grants [1, 39, 40].

2.4 Teaching and learning strategies

Findings from research are used to improve teaching and learning by promoting academic excellence using the highest international standards of teaching, learning and leadership development. This demands a series of academic quality improvement initiatives that will nurture a culture of continuous improvement and strengthen the teaching and learning experience of students and faculty. In the University of Ghana for example, relevant resources are used to enable the university meet the basic standards of internationalization through support of PhD training for cohort of lecturers without PhDs and phase out old system of lecturers without PhDs.

This was done through the following means:

1. Provide training and mentoring support for early career academics to enhance teaching and research skills.

2. Provide research support and research leadership training opportunities for mid-career academics.

3. Establish and enforce, through AQAU, standardized teaching methods for undergraduate and post-graduate teaching.

4. Enhance the importance and utility of the UG library system to the university community.

5. Establish and promote university-wide spaces and schedules for sharing and debating intra- and inter-disciplinary scholarly ideas targeted at the university community and the university's stakeholders.

6. Refurbish all lecture rooms and laboratories with updated pedagogical technology [8].

2.5 Gender and diversity

Most successful universities in Africa have created the best environment for equal opportunity in gender and diversity. These Universities recognizes the importance of Gender and Diversity and how it impacts on the social processes of inclusion and exclusion, and their interrelated demographics such as disability, religion, and ethnicity among others. In the University of Education, Winneba (UEW) for example, the Gender Directorate is created to ensure that gender and diversity are enshrined in all aspects of its institutional culture, in a manner that sets the example for all other academic and non-academic institutions to follow through these measures, evaluate and effectively implement.

In 2007 a study commissioned by Partnership for Higher Education in Africa (PHEA) mentioned that "Gender is a systemic component of all educational studies, since transformation in education, ... cannot proceed without engaging with issues of gender equity" [41]. Gender and diversity, according to the study turn to depend on "personalities and on the beliefs and perceptions they bring to their office" (p. 129). And this has governance issues and policy implications. Institutions of higher learning should have policy, strategies, and practices that resonant a clear diversity and multicultural leadership.

2.6 Monitoring and evaluation

The quality assurance division in most African university serves as the mainstream and enforces the structures and processes for system -wide monitoring and evaluation in the Public Universities in Ghana and this is mainly carried out through:

1. Creation of an effective and efficient monitoring and evaluation systems for both students and lecturers.

2. Building a strong quality assurance culture.

3. Developing a comprehensive framework for reviewing the performance of the collegiate system.

4. Developing and implement an effective framework for staff performance management.

5. Development and implementation of a monitoring and evaluation plan for the University.

6. Monitoring the achievement of internationalization in the university [42].

In summary, successful university leaders have demonstrated that strategic thinking is traditionally held in the domain of university leaders who have the primary responsibility for developing and implementing the strategic plan of the institution. Undoubtedly, Strategic thinking is a significant aspect of every leader's job: An institution may not need a strategy if it did not have to compete - it could make do simply with a plan. But strategy implies competing and outwitting competitors. In this regards leaders have to find alternative ways of competing and providing value for money. It is therefore prudent that every university has to position itself by finding alternative ways of competing with premium universities of the world.

3. The concept of governance and university governance

Ancient as it may be every society whether small or large needs to be governed. The need for governance exists anytime a group of people come together to accomplish an end. Though the governance literature proposes several definitions, most rest on three dimensions: authority, decision-making and accountability. At the higher institution level in Africa, governance determines who has power, who makes decisions, how other staff members make their voice heard and how account is rendered.

The concept has been around in both political and academic discourse for a long time, referring in a generic sense to the task of running a government, or any other appropriate entity for that matter. In this regard the general definition provided by Webster's Third New International [30] is of some assistance, indicating only that governance is a synonym for government, or "the act or process of governing, specifically authoritative direction and control". This interpretation specifically focuses on the effectiveness of the executive branch of government.

The working definition used by the British Council, however, emphasizes that "governance" is a broader notion than government (and for that matter also related concepts like the state, good government and regime), and goes on to state: "Governance involves interaction between the formal institutions and those in civil society. Governance refers to a process whereby elements in society wield power, authority and influence and enact policies and decisions concerning public life and social upliftment."

In relevance to the chapter, governance has been defined to refer to the institutional structures leadership and processes that are designed to ensure accountability, transparency, responsiveness, rule of law, stability, equity and inclusiveness, empowerment, and broad-based participation of every staff member. In higher institutions in Africa governance also represents the norms, values and rules of the game through which the institutional affairs are managed in a manner that is transparent, participatory, inclusive and responsive. Undoubtedly, institutional governance therefore can be subtle and may not be easily observable. In a broad sense, governance is about the culture and institutional environment in which citizens and stakeholders interact among themselves and participate in public affairs. It is more than the organs of the government.

International agencies such as UNDP, the World Bank, the OECD, Development Assistance Committee (DAC) and others define governance as the exercise of authority or power in order to manage a country's economic, political and administrative affairs. The [43] sees governance as 'power relationships,' 'formal and informal processes of formulating policies and allocating resources,' 'processes of decision-making' and 'mechanisms for holding governments accountable.'

Recently, in Africa, the terms "governance" and "good governance" are being increasingly used in development literature because of the way and manner African universities have been politicized by Africa leaders. The ripple effects has seen most of the Public Universities in Ghana and other African countries having leaders who were corrupt and made unproductive decision-making which has gone a long way to affect productivity in most universities. Bad governance (which is the opposite of good governance) is being increasingly regarded as one of the root causes of all evil within in most African universities. At the University level "governance" is a means through which senior members such as the Vice-Chancellor, Pro-Vice-Chancellor and the Registrar who are the three most senior members make decisions, implement them, direct and control their functions. These roles help those in charge to relate to their stakeholders in order to achieve the mission and vision of the institution.

It is important to note that after independence, the state or government of various African countries were given total control over the highest learning institution. In this regard, public financing coupled with oversight, appointment and control of the organizational structure of higher learning institutions during this era was common. Most often, heads of states becoming chancellor of major state universities in Africa. This made access to higher educational institutions limited under the system with quotas on admission due to limited funds. However, demands of the citizens with pressure from groups and individuals with influence forced expansion of the system, with funding still a prevalent problem. The pressure of expansion resulted in enlargement, proliferation and diversification of providers and increase in the mode of delivery. In this process, the states turn out to be one of the providers of higher learning rather than managing higher learning in the African continent.

If the notion of institutional governance encompasses how power is distributed and shared, how policies are formulated, priorities set and stakeholders made accountable then it evidently clear that institutional governance are challenged with the following:

1. Effective representation of diverse students and staff

2. Aging teaching and non-teaching staff

3. Organizational climate and change

4. Technologies and innovation

5. Accountability, transparency, and probity

6. Student, staff and community participation [39, 40, 42]

3.1 University governance: the case of selected universities in Africa

Universities worldwide exist for purpose not different to other universities in any other country. It is assumed that universities of the globe exist for simple purpose of effective teaching, research and community engagement. On numerous occasions it is argued that the role of an African university is not clearly articulated within the African context because of the borrowed curriculum used by these universities in

Africa. For example, [44] were doubtful with regard to the capacity of African universities to carry out academic projects with their problems to manage contradictory functions of political ideologies and academic activities. Notwithstanding, the former UN Secretary General Kofi Annan argued that Universities in Africa must become a primary tool for Africa's development in the new century. Bloom and Reenen [45] posit that universities can aid in the development of African expertise; they can enhance the analysis of African problems; strengthen domestic institutions; serve as model environment for the practice of good governance, conflict resolution and respect for human rights, and enable African academics to play an active part in the global community of scholars.

If these objectives are to be achieved in African universities, research and community engagement have to be well-conceived and emphasized by various university management rather than making teaching the only known function of African developing university [1]. Sebola [46] argues that the business purpose of a university (teaching, research, community engagement) is unique and does not need to be compromised. The lack of attention by leadership to the other two reasons of existence have indeed made the role of some African university no different from a high school or a further education and training institution (now called Technical Vocational Education Centers). This explains a poor scientific publication output by African universities which according to [47], contribute less than 1% of the global scientific publications. This has been a worrisome factor for long in academic discourses as to why Africans are only labeled consumers of knowledge than being producers of it. The answer to these and other worrisome factors are due to the fact that most African universities leaders lack the skills to think and manage strategically.

The success of each society is mainly based on its educated workforce that aims to contribute to economic growth and social prosperity [48, 49]. Undoubtedly, highly-skilled workforce produced at universities will be able to solve economic problems through the knowledge and research skills obtained from African universities. But on the contrary studies have shown that most African universities through their leadership (governance) have proven negligence by providing a knowledge, skills and competency mismatch that do not meet employer profiles [48, 50]. In this regard, [1] advocate that universities in Africa should make their visions and missions well known to all stakeholders rather than monopolizing them.

In most instances the African university leadership claims to operate on good governance principles but on the contrary they have created an artificial blockage between themselves and all other internal stakeholders such as staff, students and labor unions. Most of their activities seem to be shrouded in secrecy. Hence it is argued that the concept governance itself may not be a problem in African universities, because [51] argues that developing a good governance strategies among internal stakeholder may lead to the success of good governance model workable to achieve successful African university businesses. Good governance recognizes that those in authority cannot exclude the stakeholders in issues that need engagement before decisions are undertaken [52].

The high demand for higher learning in Africa by a teeming youth with a desire to improve on their knowledge created a large market for higher educational institution in Africa and this is evident by the wide spread of private universities with other public institutions being privatized. Government of various African countries, especially Ghana, saw the need to enact new laws for the management and control of the public and private universities. Some of these included granting autonomy to the universities, creating regulatory bodies, programming and maintaining standard, external quality assurance mechanisms to help in the governance of universities and upgrading of Polytechnics to university status.

If these objectives are to be achieved in Africa, and Ghana for that matter, then it is bent on leadership to formulate policies, actions and plans to achieve the visions of the universities through strategic plan, road map and actions to be undertaken to achieve their targets with the new university legislations, defining the roles and responsibilities of government, regulatory bodies among others, consequently replacing head of states as chancellors with prominent scholars, Chief Executive officers and vice chancellors.

Due to the high demand for university education in Africa, some institutions have developed courses which may have no relevance to the students, school and the country as a whole. These courses are just seen as "money making" for the universities. Students who graduate from these courses have no jobs and little to contribute to the society. For example, Cape Town University has before time planned for courses to be offered in the 2020 academic year looking at what situation demands in their community and country. The success story to be learned here is that courses should not just be introduced for 'money-making' but rather the courses pursued should have impact on the community and the country as a whole. In University of Education, for example, the blending of education and business courses such as Banking and Finance, Procurement, Marketing, Purchasing and Supply Chain introduced in 2015/2016 academic year has enabled student to gain employment both as qualified teacher and entrepreneurs.

3.1.1 Leadership and governance in African universities

In Ghana and for that matter most African country, universities are established based on legal status. In Ghana, for example, all the Public Universities were established by an Act. For example, the University of Ghana was established by the University of Ghana Act, 1961 (Act 79) to replace the then University College of Ghana. The Act was amended in 2010 by the University of Ghana Act, 2010 (Act 806). All the Public Universities in Ghana are considered as a corporate with a legal personality and can sue and be sued in its own name. University of Ghana, Kwame Nkrumah University of Science and Technology, University of Cape Coast and University of Education, are all governed by the University Council members appointed by the Government whose duties include but are not limited to determining the strategic direction of the University, promoting means of generating income for the university and appointing professors to the University.

The University Council is also responsible for the management and administration of the finances and properties of the University. Council also has general control over the affairs and public relations of the University including the use of the common seal of the University. The Vice Chancellor is the academic and administrative head and chief disciplinary officer of the University, while the Registrar is the chief operating officer responsible for the day to day administration of the affairs of the University. The Office of the Vice-Chancellor in most Public Universities in Ghana coordinates all the major activities of the University. The office basically comprises the Pro-Vice-Chancellor and the Vice-Chancellor's offices.

3.2 Lessons for successful universities in Africa

If Strategic thinking and leadership is needed for a creative endeavor and a dynamic, responsive change to influence the change of governance in most African universities, then [1] argue that the possibility lies through the emergence of both developing strategic thinking skills among leaders in African universities, this to a large extent encourage professionalism and responsiveness to societal needs. Through interviews with 12 African University leaders (both past and current)

DOI: http://dx.doi.org/10.5772/intechopen.81196

it was clear that the success of African universities lies in the following practices including organizational trust, student participation and stakeholder's involvement.

In an effort to govern successfully universities in Africa, one is tempted to offer a word of caution by repeating what by Wayne Turmel in 2007: Avoid governing with BIG 'L' entitlement:

> *These are the people who are in positions of authority –leaders in a company. They are "Big L" leaders. They're expected to lead because that's what their job title says they do. After all, if you're paid more than me and have a more impressive title, I'd like to assume that you're leading the parade.*

Leadership is everything; leaders chart uncharted courses; and if leadership is the cause, then all others are effects.

3.2.1 Organizational trust

According to [53], trust is analyzed in two categories: trust among individuals, and trust in abstract systems. In its broadest meaning, organizational trust is the dispositional beliefs that employees have for their organizations [54]. Organizational trust also reflects the perceptions of an employee related to the support provided by the organization [55]. Taylor [56] points out that organizational trust is a phenomenon developed through harmonious behavior based on mutual respect and courtesy, and is realized over time. This implies that for University leadership to develop organizational trust among staff member, they must respect and give their members the due courtesy and vice versa.

This implies that leadership and staff members who work together in the University ought to have a trusting work relationship because if they do not trust one another, they are not likely to disclose information openly to each other. The issues of transparency, openness, accountability and democracy are some of the factors of most successful universities across the globe. Newcombe and McCormick [57] points out that the desire to be involved or not to be involved in the decision-making may stem from lack of trust in the decision makers and the decision-making processes which at the university level is the beginning of successful leadership.

3.2.2 Students participation

The inclusion of students in the management of Universities in Africa is long overdue. It will be argued that all the universities in Africa have Student Representative Council (SRC) Members who serve on the University Council and mediate between students and the universities. It time for University management to recognize that without these students there will not be any institutions called University. Lesson learned from successful universities in Africa indicate for African universities to be successful, the involvement of students in decision-making is important at the tertiary level [1]. Most successful universities across the globe have demonstrated that student participation in decision-making may lead to increase in academic performance and decrease in indiscipline among university students. However, the bureaucratic structures that exit in most African universities challenges barely make student participation flourish.

Observational studies in most Ghanaian Universities have shown that university student leaders are constantly threatened whenever they tend to disagree with university authorities. It is however, worthwhile to note that some university leadership still monopolize decision-making despite available literature that replete with known and huge benefits to be derived from participatory decision-making.

It is worrisome that University leadership who ought to know better about the best leadership styles for achieving optimal student participation for goal attainment are still excluding students from some aspects of school decision-making. Students, in particular, are the recipients of the core business in universities; therefore, their contributions assist in the discussion of pedagogical matters and other matters which directly affect them which is why they need to be involved in the management of the universities.

3.2.3 Stakeholders involvement

The term "stakeholders" has become fashionable in many African countries, including Ghana, Nigeria and South Africa. The term is based on the assumption that certain groups and individuals have an interest, or a "stake" in the activities of an institution. According to [58] the stakeholders are all those people who have a legitimate interest in the continuing effectiveness and success of an institution. In contextualizing this definition, one gets a picture of an ideal situation where various stakeholders in a university setting (parents, lectures, business entities, learners, government, community) come together and make decisions in pursuit of a common interest. This fashionable idea of stakeholders' involvement poses a challenge for institutional leaders in most African universities in regard of their skills and capacities as they have to adopt more collaborative and inclusive decision-making processes.

Research into the ever-changing institutional environment and the dynamic roles of University leadership clearly shows that there is now a far greater focus on their interpersonal skills and capabilities, since they are now required to lead the whole institutional community while facilitating participation and collaboration among stakeholders in decision-making, planning and budgeting, their leadership skills and capacities are critical [38]. This implies that to avoid making sole, arbitrary, and emotional decisions that are detrimental to optimum goal attainment, the University leadership should gather all available data or information concerning institutional related issues to be decided upon and make most effective use of available data by sharing with staff and all concerned stakeholders. This becomes easier and possible when the leaders taps from the ideas, knowledge, opinions, and suggestions from all stakeholders and make them understand that their inputs count in making administrative decisions.

Additionally, existing literature advocate for the following as pillars supporting successful African universities.

1. Using Information and Communication Technologies effectively for instructional delivery, professional communication, to develop, produce, acquire and distribute knowledge, skills and competencies across the continent as fast as they are available;

2. Building human resource base that will seek newer and effective ways to combat diseases, reduce energy costs and address climate change;

3. Creating centers of excellence within each region of the continent to develop robust postgraduate studies and develop strong research base with global competitive advantage; and,

4. Seeking opportunities for collaboration and partnership on equal and mutually beneficial platforms with the international world including universities in other continents, development partners, organization and agencies genuinely interested in higher education in Africa.

5. Prioritizing what matters. When working on content, much time should be spent on crafting wonderful headlines, finding great photo and writing a good caption. This may be a more effective strategy than spending too much time on the body copy. The header and image will be responsible for turning a scanner into a reader. Without a grabbing headline, no one is going to read the body copy.

6. Risk taking. Always challenge the status quo and measure energy when a new idea is introduced. Look for ideas that get people talking. In some cases, it can be red flag sign when everyone loves your work. It means it is too familiar, too safe and too comfortable to make a memorable difference.

7. Strategically planning the objectives of the school. Planning the objectives of the school should cover years to come and working towards achieving those objectives.

8. Keeping doors open for new opportunities.

9. Giving back to the society in which the school operates. By so doing, the school reaps back the financial rewards.

In conclusion, [1] argue that the following lessons can be learned from successful universities:

- A policy should be designed to augment the status of all universities to concentrate on applied research and innovation towards industries. The marriage between academic research and industry should be exemplary. The policy should spell out financial incentives for research and entrepreneurship within the Universities and a strong collaboration among academics and students.

- There should also be a strategic plan to encourage synergy between academic researchers and industries in Ghana. Part of the policy is to award scholarship and reward innovations among TU institutes. Practicable policies should be developed to encourage technical training, vocational competencies, and non-traditional academic pursuits among children right from the basic level of education to solve problems related to the society.

Author details

Dandy George Dampson* and Alexander Kyei Edwards
University of Education, Winneba, Ghana

*Address all correspondence to: dgdampson@gmail.com

References

[1] Edwards AK, Raheem K, Dampson DG. Strategic thinking and strategic leadership for change: Lessons for technical universities in Ghana. Malaysian Online Journal of Educational Management. 2017;**6**(1):53-67

[2] Anamuah-Mensah J, Wolfenden F. TESSA OER: A Sustainable Approach to Teacher Education in Sub-Saharan Africa. Accra, Ghana: Association of African Universities; 2009

[3] Naituli G, Kronlid DO. Rethinking University Education in Kenya: The Case for ESD in Higher Education. Accra, Ghana: Association of African Universities; 2009

[4] Urama KC. Higher Education for Sustainable Development in Africa. Accra, Ghana: Association of African Universities; 2009

[5] Appiah-Adu K, Aning S. Enhancing government's policy management and decision-making system: The case of Ghana's central governance reforms project. Canadian Public Administration. 2012;**55**(1):125-147

[6] Edwards AK, Sam FK. Strategic thinking with 'Brain Powers' by considering leadership in appreciative inquiry. Global Education Review. 2014;**2**(4):58-67

[7] Stringham S. Strategic Leadership and Strategic Management: Leading and Managing Change on the Edge of Chaos. Bloomington: iUniverse; 2012

[8] NCTE Technical Report. Stakeholders Consultative Forum on the Conversion of Polytechnics to Technical Universities. Accra, Ghana: Ministry of Education; 2015. Available from: http://ncte.edu.gh/images/pdf/st.pdf [Accessed: May 1, 2016]

[9] Jelenc L. The impact of strategic management schools and strategic thinking on the performance of Croatian entrepreneurial practice [unpublished PhD dissertation]. University of Ljubljana; 2008

[10] Liedtka JM, Rosenblum JW. Teaching strategy as design: A report from the field. Journal of Management Education. 1998;**22**(3):285-303

[11] Rosche ALHW. Personality Correlates of Strategic Thinking in an Organizational Context. San Francisco Bay: Alliant International University, California School of Organizational Studies; 2003

[12] Fairholm MR, Fairholm GW. Understanding Leadership Perspectives: Theoretical and Practical Approaches. New York: Springer Science & Business Media; 2009

[13] Bonn I. Developing strategic thinking as a core competency. Management Decision. 2001;**39**(1):63-71

[14] Goldman EF. Strategic thinking at the top. MIT Sloan Management Review. 2007;**48**(4):75

[15] Liedtka JM. Strategic thinking: Can it be taught? Long Range Planning. 1998;**31**(1):120-129

[16] Mintzberg H. The fall and rise of strategic planning. Harvard Business Review. 1994;**72**(1):107-114

[17] Goldman EF. Leadership practices that encourage strategic thinking. Journal of Strategy and Management. 2012;**5**(1):25-40

[18] Haycock K, Cheadle A, Bluestone KS. Strategic thinking.

Library Leadership & Management. 2012;**26**(93/4):1-23

[19] Markides C. Think again: Fine-tuning your strategic thinking. Business Strategy Review. 2012;**23**(4):80-85

[20] Graetz F. Strategic thinking versus strategic planning: Towards understanding the complementarities. Management Decision. 2002;**40**(5):456-462

[21] Nicholson WD II. Leading where it counts: An investigation of the leadership styles and behaviors that define college and university presidents as successful fundraisers. International Journal of Educational Advancement. 2007;7(4):256-270

[22] Kouzes JM, Posner BZ. LPI: Leadership Practices Inventory: Development Planner. San Francisco: John Wiley & Sons; 2012

[23] Morrill RL. Strategic Leadership: Integrating Strategy and Leadership in Colleges and Universities. Lanham: Rowman & Littlefield Publishers; 2010

[24] Balogun J, Hailey VH. Exploring Strategic Change. London: Pearson Education; 2008

[25] Sharma P, Chrisman SJJ. Toward a reconciliation of the definitional issues in the field of corporate entrepreneurship. In: Entrepreneurship. Berlin, Heidelberg: Springer; 2007. pp. 83-103

[26] Murphy L, de Larios JR. Searching for words: One strategic use of the mother tongue by advanced Spanish EFL writers. Journal of Second Language Writing. 2010;**19**(2):61-81

[27] Baumol WJ. Entrepreneurship: Productive, unproductive, and destructive. The Journal of Political Economy. 2006;**98**(5):893-921

[28] Edoho FM. Entrepreneurship paradigm and economic renaissance in Africa. African Journal of Economic and Management Studies. 2015;**6**(1):2-16

[29] Scholarship of Engagement. Introduction. Available from: http://www.scholarshipof engagement.org/evaluation/evaluation_criteria.html [Accessed: April 15, 2016]

[30] Dictionary.com. Online Dictionary. Available from: http://www.dictionary.com [Accessed: May 2nd, 2016]

[31] Edwards, AK. Professional citizenship and otherness leadership development: Examining the relationships among meaning, moral reasoning, and diversity competencies of graduate students [doctoral dissertation]. OH, USA: Bowling Green State University; 2009

[32] Wilkins M. Reasserting professionalism: A polemic. In: Smith JFR, editor. The Role of Higher Education in Initial Teacher Training. London, UK: Kogan Page; 2009. pp. 139-150

[33] Feurer R, Chaharbaghi K. Strategy development: Past, present and future. Training for Quality. 1997;**5**(2):58-70

[34] Griffin RW. Management. USA: Houghton Mifflin Company; 2004

[35] Alashloo FR, Castka P, Sharp JM. Towards understanding the impeders of strategy implementation in higher education (HE), a case of HE Institutes in Iran. Quality Assurance in Education. 2005;**13**(2):132-147

[36] Brewer PD, Brewer VL, Hawksley M. Strategic planning for continuous improvement in a College of Business. The Mid-Atlantic Journal of Business. 2000;**36**(2-3):123-132

[37] Ellis S, Dick P. Introduction to Organizational Behaviour. London: McGraw-Hill; 2000

[38] Dampson DG. Teacher participation in decision-making in Ghanaian basic schools: A study of some selected schools in the Cape Coast metropolitan area and the Mfantseman municipality in the Central Region of Ghana [unpublished thesis]. Submitted to the School of Education, University of Northampton, UK for an Award of PhD. 2015

[39] University of Education. Vice Chancellor's Annual Report. Winneba, Ghana: University Press; 2015

[40] Cape Coast, Ghana: University Press; Available from: https://www.ucc.edu.gh. [Accessed: May 2nd, 2016]

[41] Manuh T, Gariba S, Budu J. Change and transformation in Ghana's publicly funded universities. In: Partnership for Higher Education in Africa. Oxford, UK/Ghana: James Currey and Accra/ Woeli Publishing Services; 2007

[42] University of Ghana Statutes. The Statutes of the University of Ghana. Vol. 24/52. Legon: Ghana Universities Press; 2004. pp. 2-6

[43] Global Monitoring Report. Accountability in Education. 2016. Available from: www.unesco.org

[44] Cloete N, Maassen P. Knowledge Production and Contradictory Functions in African Higher Education. Cape Town: African Minds; 2015. p. 2015

[45] Bloom N, Reenen VR. Measuring and explaining management practices across firms and countries. Quarterly Journal of Economics. 2007;**122**(4):203-224

[46] Sebola MP. The politicisation of government administration: The limited "brutal" options of the south African government administration. Mediterranean Journal of Social Sciences. 2014;**5**(7):208

[47] Karlan D, Valdivia M. Teaching enterpreneurship: Impact of business training on microfinance client and institutions. Review of Economics and Statistics. 2011;**93**(2):510-527

[48] Bloom N, Eifert B, Aprajit M, McKenzie D, Roberts J. Does management matter? Evidence from India. The Quarterly Journal of Economics. 2013;**1**:51

[49] Sebola MP, Malema PW. South African teachers' perception of integrated quality management systems: Mopani District Secondary Schools, Limpopo Province. Journal of Social Sciences. 2014;**41**(2):233-242

[50] Du Preez I, Fossey A. Developing academic writing skills as part of graduate attributes in undergraduate curricula. South African Journal of Higher Education. 2012;**26**(2): 346-357

[51] Naidoo B, Perumal J. Female prinicipals leading at disadvantage schools in Johannesberg, South Africa. Educational Administration and Management. 2014;**42**(6):808-824

[52] Nambalirwa S, Sindane AM. Governance and public leadership: The missing links in service delivery in South Africa. Journal of Public Administration. 2012;**47**(3):695-705

[53] Giddens A. Sociology. 2nd ed. Cambridge: Polity Press; 1996

[54] Zaheer A, Mcevily B, Percone V. Does trust matter? Exploring the effects inter-organizational and interpersonal trust on performance. Organization Science. 1998;**9**:141-159

[55] Mishra J, Morrissey MA. Trust in employee/employer relationships: A survey of West Michigan managers. Public Personnel Management. 1990;**19**(4):443-486

[56] Taylor RG. The role of trust In labor-management relations. Organization Development Journal. 1989;**7**:85-89

[57] Newcombe G, McCormick J. Trust and teacher participation in school based financial management. Educational Management Administration and Leadership. 2001;**29**(2):181-195

[58] Bush T, Heystek J. School governance in the new South Africa. Compare. 2003;**33**(2):127-138

Section 3

On Dynamic Capabilities

Chapter 4

Evaluation of Property Management Agent Performance: A Novel Empirical Model

Yung Yau and Daniel Chi Wing Ho

Abstract

For many different reasons, property management agents (PMAs) are appointed for managing housing developments in both public and private housing sectors in many different cities. While third-party housing management eases the burdens of property owners and tenants in taking care of their properties, it may lead to agency problems. In fact, cases of mismanagement of multi-owned properties are common in Hong Kong and other Asian cities, leading to accelerated urban decay and augmented confrontations between property owners, users and PMAs. To promote better property management services, the performance of PMAs should be evaluated so market players can benchmark the performance of different PMAs for better-informed decision-making. This study reviews previous and existing measures for evaluating PMA performance and proposes a new evaluation model which is built upon the residual concept proposed by William Sharpe. The ideas underpinning the framework and how a PMA's performance is evaluated using the framework are detailed. Using this new model, 217 housing developments in Hong Kong are studied and the performance of the respective PMAs is evaluated and benchmarked. The evaluation outcomes are validated with the SERVQUAL scores of these 217 housing developments. Practical implications of the research findings follow.

Keywords: residual concept, performance evaluation, benchmarking, agency problems, property management agents, building stock management

1. Introduction

Strategic management is a very broad field accommodating literature focusing on strategy [1–3] and processes of strategy formulation and implementation [4–7]. It was branched out from management science into a new discipline in the 1960s [8]. Later, "strategic management" was once a big buzzword in the business sector in the 1970s and 1980s. While a large volume of literature has been contributed to the knowledge of corporate strategy, strategic management is still of little relevance to other disciplines, particularly urban and building studies. In fact, the principles and tools of strategic management can be employed in urban management to achieve the goal of urban sustainability [9, 10]. Given that there is a close link between quality of housing and life quality of residents, it is very important to make sure that our housing stock is properly managed. Identification of good performers and poor performers can help different stakeholders, including homeowners, property management agents (PMAs) and public authorities, to make more informed decisions on the management of the housing stock in a city. In this chapter, we focus on two particular aspects of strategic management – performance measurement and benchmarking – in the arena of MOH management. We propose a new way to evaluate and benchmark the performance of PMAs in management of multi-owned housing (MOH) in high-rise cities. Hong Kong is taken as a case for illustrating the proposed paradigm.

2. MOH management: importance and challenges

MOH comes in many different forms such as apartments, condominiums and common interest developments [11]. MOH has gained its popularity in many high-rise Asian cities like Hong Kong, Kuala Lumpur, Shanghai, Singapore and Taipei. Compared with the case of single-family houses, management of MOH is more complicated. In a typical MOH development, common parts (or communal parts), including water pumps, underground sewers, lifts, service ducts, staircases, access corridors, lift lobbies and entrance halls, are co-owned. Owing to their co-ownership nature, these common or co-owned parts pose challenges in housing management as the associated management responsibility has to be shared by all homeowners [11]. In addition to the operation and use of the tangible, physical building fabrics and services, vigilant MOH management also needs to observe many other intangible aspects like security, quietness and environmental hygiene within the housing development. Proper management is crucial for assuring the quality of the residential environment and residents' well-being in the long run in several ways [12, 13]. First, it is conducive to the vigilant upkeep of the physical built environment and better built environment in turn safeguards the residents' health. Empirical evidence has shown that compared with those mismanaged or unmanaged, buildings which are properly managed have better safety and hygienic performance [14, 15]. Second, good MOH management can reduce neighbor conflicts and disputes by regulating the behavior of the residents (e.g. prohibiting littering in communal areas). Third, from the economic perspective, proper building maintenance can slow down value depreciation of the housing assets and preserve property value [16, 17]. Fourth, apposite MOH management facilitates timely building maintenance and repair which prolongs the serviceable lives of housing assets and relaxes the pressing need for redevelopment [18]. Accordingly, this reduces demolition and construction waste and eases the problem of resident displacement, going along with the principles of environmental and social sustainability.

On account of the technicality of building systems and services and large number of co-owners involved in MOH developments, particularly those high-rise ones, it is often not an unchallenging task for layman homeowners to manage their own MOH developments. Apart from a high level of cooperation among co-owners, effective management of MOH developments requires a lot of manpower and professional skills [19, 20]. Taking the very situation in MOH management into consideration, different parties such as professional bodies, scholars and governments advocate the engagement of a third-party or external property management agent (PMA) for managing a MOH development on the owners' behalf or in collaboration with the owners [14, 21, 22]. In Hong Kong, management services of an estimated 60% of apartment developments are entirely or partly outsourced to external PMAs.

As a matter of fact, MOH management has many similarities with corporate management. In a MOH development, the committee of a homeowner association (which can be named in different ways such as body corporate, owners' corporation, condominium association or strata committee) is analogous to board of directors in a company. On the other hand, the roles played by a PMA in MOH management are similar to those of a chief executive officer (CEO) in a company. The PMA (CEO) must keep the homeowners (shareholders) satisfied, make sure the housing development (company) running smoothly, oversee support staff and make regular reports to the homeowners (shareholders) and homeowner association (board of directors). Yet, relationship between the board of directors and CEO is vulnerable to the classical principal-agent problems because of the diverse incentives of the two parties [23–25]. The same also occurs in the case of MOH management [26–28]. It is very common that PMAs act for their own benefits at the homeowners' expense. Opportunistic PMAs may embezzle fund from the common financial pool (such as sinking fund and maintenance reserve) to their own pockets or make procurement decisions on their own instead of the homeowners. These malpractices of the PMAs have been widely reported in different parts of the world [29–32]. In this light, different measures have been devised or institutionalized to regulate PMAs' practices. For example, a property management license is needed for property managers in many states of the United States [33]. A new licensing regime for the property managers will be also in place in Hong Kong soon [34].

Aside from the regulation, principal-agent problems can be mitigated to a certain extent by offering market information or signals to the market players. In the arena of MOH management, a particular piece of information that the market players need to know in their decision-making processes is the PMA's performance. Therefore, measurement and benchmarking of performance of PMAs in MOH management are of paramount importance in the strategic management of housing stock in a city. Given that the PMAs' performance can be benchmarked, homeowners can be better informed in PMA selection for management of their MOH developments. PMAs themselves can also know their own performance relative to their competitors. Against this backdrop, we propose a framework for evaluating and comparing performance of PMAs in MOH management in Hong Kong in this chapter.

3. Measurement and benchmarking of PMA's performance

Performance measurement and benchmarking are essential elements of strategic management [35]. While there has been a large body of literature on benchmarking in the field of business management, little attention has been paid to benchmarking of housing or property management performance.

3.1 Existing performance indicators or measures

With a relatively short history, research on performance measurement or evaluation of property or housing management services started in the mid-1980s. In the very beginning, social housing was the main focus of research [36]. Over the past 30 years, various key performance indicators were employed or suggested in the literature for measuring or evaluating a PMA's performance. These performance indicators or measures can be broadly classified into four types, namely input-based measures, output-based measures, process-based measures, and hybrid measures. This categorization is based on the premise that provision of property management service can be analogous to industrial production. In industrial production, we put in different resources in various amounts to produce a quantity of our desired products. The products are then purchased and consumed or used by customers to enhance their wellbeing. The resources we dedicate in the production process are the "inputs" which can be capital, raw materials and labor. In property management, in order to provide the service, PMAs have to put in labor and expertise. That is why monthly headcount of direct personnel involved in daily property management process, hours of staff training and professional development, and number of professional licenses a PMA has are common input-based performance measures for property management [37].

As for the "outputs", they generally refer to the products of the production process. In the case of property management, output-based measures concern the outputs can be the amount of service provided by a PMA or the assessable outcomes of property management process [38]. Frequencies of management activities (such as security patrol and cleansing of communal lobbies and corridors) within a specified time period are used as typical key performance indicators. Yet, these indicators represent the "immediate outputs" of the service provision of property management. Unlike manufacturing of consumer goods, the service provided by different PMAs is unlikely to be homogeneous even though they clean a building at the same frequency. Thus we need to recognize and identify the variations in the quality of property management service. In this light, it is also sensible to consider the "final outputs" which are the consequential effects or outcomes after the use of the service by the consumer. In property management, these final outputs can be the level of resident satisfaction and actual physical conditions of the MOH development.

Process-based performance measurement is key element in benchmarking which drives corporates and service providers to follow best practices in their fields [39]. With many variants, process-based measures focus on the operation process of PMAs. For instance, possession of certifications from the International Organization for Standardization (ISO) such as ISO9001 and ISO10002 is a common process-based measure in the property management sector [40–42]. In addition, whether specific practices (e.g. documentations and thoughtful emergency planning) are taken when managing a property can indicate PMA's performance [43].

Actually, input-based, output-based and process-based measures are not mutually exclusively. They can be used together to form some hybrid measures which typically come in a form of multi-attribute evaluation tool [44, 45]. However, the four measures aforementioned have their own weaknesses. For instance, input-based performance evaluation tends to overlook the service outcomes. In many cases, homeowners concern the management outcomes such as security level and environmental hygiene more than the management inputs. On the other hand, output-based measures ignore key factors affecting the outcomes of property management. Intrinsic characteristics of a housing development could be one of the examples of these overlooked factors. For example, the decent condition of a MOH development is probably the natural result of the young age of the property rather than the PMA's real efforts paid in housing management.

Regarding process-based measurement, its similarity with a traditional check-and-tick practice is not favorable to service innovation. In order to secure a high performance score, a PMA can make reference to a prescriptive checklist and adopt all the practices enlisted. There is no need to invest in or adopt innovative practices which lead to good performance. As for the hybrid measures, they seems to be the most convincing approach. Nonetheless, there are often debates on what factors, indicators or attributes should be incorporated into the evaluation system or framework. Given that the choices of attributes can be quite scenario-specific, hybrid measures may not be able to offer genuine apple-to-apple comparison of the performance across PMAs. A set of performance attributes that are more relevant to large-scale MOH developments may not be applicable to small-scale ones.

No matter which type of performance measure is used, it is crucial that only the component of performance that is controllable by PMA should be accounted for. Akin to what has been discussed before, it would be inapt to attribute a more pleasant environment and better physical condition of a MOH development to better performance of its PMA without holding other exogenous factors constant. This is a zone that the literature has yet to address. In this regard, a more rigorous and generalized method to evaluate the PMA performance in MOH management is needed.

3.2 New paradigm for evaluating and benchmarking PMAs' performance

To reiterate, we aim to propose a new paradigm for measuring and comparing the performance of PMAs in providing professional property management service to the homeowners of MOH developments in this chapter. The proposed paradigm is designed to allow the performance to be assessed in a *ceteris paribus* condition (i.e. holding other exogenous variables constant). In the paradigm, management performance of a PMA is defined as the achievement of the PMA in managing the MOH development such that the residents are satisfied with the living environment and the MOH development is maintained in a good condition. In fact, this definition is justifiable because professional property management service provided by PMAs have dual dimensions – namely the tangible and intangible dimensions. Tangible dimension concerns the upkeep of the physical condition of the development which is an important indicator in PMA performance evaluation as most homeowners employ a PMA with an expectation that the environmental hygiene and safety of their housing developments can be safeguarded. Intangible dimension, on the other hand, includes how PMAs deliver their services to the residents.

How much does a PMA contribute to the good (or poor) condition of a MOH development? Similarly, how much does a PMA contribute to the high (or low) level of residential satisfaction within a MOH development? Regarding these two questions, the true contribution of the PMA to the physical condition and residential satisfaction of the development cannot be ascertained directly or explicitly. Therefore, resort is made to an indirect measurement. As a matter of fact, the role of a PMA in MOH management can be, to a large extent, analogous to the role of a CEO in corporate management. Both PMA and CEO serve their respective clients or principals (i.e. homeowners and boards of directors) in return for a fee-for-service. Upon this premise, we propose a residual concept for evaluating the performance of a PMA following the idea of William Sharpe [46]. As illustrated in **Figure 1**, PMA's performance is believed to be one of the factors affecting existing physical condition and residential satisfaction of a MOH development. Nevertheless, there are other factors affecting building condition and residential satisfaction. For example, inborn characteristics of a MOH development such as building age and types of material used may affect the degree of wear and tear and durability of the building fabrics, which will in turn determine the level of maintenance required for the housing development. Besides, works of a PMA may be held up or aided by different coordination mechanisms among homeowners (e.g. whether a homeowner association exists or not). Moreover, the characteristics of the residents (e.g. income and education levels) may bear impacts on the building condition because these factors affect how the common areas and facilities of a MOH development are used. All in all, these three groups of exogenous factors are assumed to exhaust all the determinants of building condition that are beyond the control of management. In

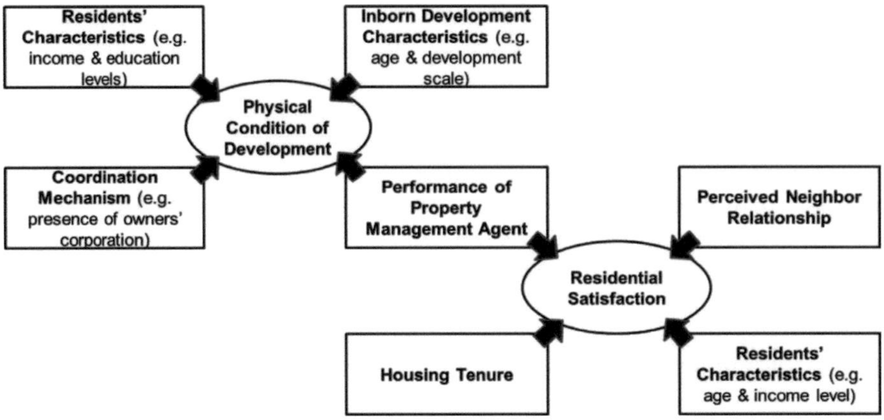

Figure 1.
Factors affecting building condition and residential satisfaction.

this sense, we can extract the PMA's efforts from the building condition by holding other exogenous factors constant.

After collection of data from a pool of MOH developments, a regression model is established to relate a MOH development's physical condition (PC) with its inborn attributes (IA), residents' characteristics (RC) and features of coordination mechanism (CM) based on the conceptual framework in **Figure 1**. Mathematically,

$$PC = f(IA, RC, CM) + \varepsilon \quad (1)$$

where f is a mathematical function to be determined; and ε is the error term, which is also called the residual. The advantage of using regression is that other factors can be held constant. Most importantly, the residual series ε specified in Eq. (1) captures implicitly the performance of the PMAs in managing their respective MOH developments. The residual accounts for the variations in building condition that cannot be explained by the exogenous factors incorporated in the model. Given the same building inborn attributes, residents' characteristics and coordination mechanism features, the differences in the physical condition of different housing developments, if any, should be attributed to the variations in the performance of PMAs managing these developments. In other words, the residual series ε measures the extent to which management performance of a PMA is higher or low than that of PMAs under similar circumstances. Likewise, as **Figure 1** shows, the overall satisfaction of the residents with the living environment of a MOH development (RS) is contingent not only on the PMA's performance. It may also be affected by the residents' demographic characteristics (DC) like age and income level, housing tenure type (HT) such as renter, owner-occupier or investor and general perception of neighbor relationship within the housing development (NR). The PMA's performance can be extracted from the residual series γ of regression results of the following equation:

$$RS = g(DC, HT, NR) + \gamma \quad (2)$$

A property management performance index (PMPI) for a PMA with respect to a particular MOH development m managed by the PMA can be computed with the following formula:

$$PMPI = \varepsilon_m + \gamma_m \quad (3)$$

where ε_m and γ_m are extracted from the residual series of Eqs. (1) and (2) respectively. The PMPI can be used to evaluate and benchmark management performance of the PMAs.

4. Benchmarking PMA performance in Hong Kong

For the purpose of illustration, the performance of selected MOH developments in Hong Kong was measured using the framework outlined above.

4.1 Measures of the variables

To operationalize the extraction of a PMA's performance in management of a MOH development from building condition, the physical condition of the MOH development (PC) was assessed using the Building Condition Index (BCI) [47]. The BCI is a multi-attribute assessment indicator of the existing condition of private multi-story residential developments, specifically-designed for the Hong Kong's context. To compile the BCI for a particular MOH development, various condition aspects including environmental hygiene, structural integrity, fire safety and presence of unauthorized appendages were rated in accordance with the respective pre-determined rating scales. The BCI ranged from 0 (for the worst scenario) to 100 (for the best scenario). As for residential satisfaction (RS), it was measured by asking a resident to indicate if his or her residential development was a good place to live using a five-point scale (1 = a very poor place to live; 2 = a poor place to live; 3 = a fair place to live; 4 = a good place to live; 5 = a very good place to live) [48]. A higher rating denoted a greater degree of residential satisfaction. An aggregate level of residential satisfaction for a MOH development was obtained by taking an arithmetic mean of all individual residential satisfaction scores.

Residents' characteristics of a MOH development were indicated using the official census data. Apart from the median monthly domestic household income (INC) and median age of the residents (RAGE), education profile of the residents (EDU) was also included in the measurement. It was measured as the percentage of population aged 15 and over in the MOH development with post-secondary education attainment. Housing tenure (TEN) was indicated by the percentage of households in a MOH development that were owner-occupiers. Regarding inborn building characteristics, age of a MOH development (DAGE) was taken as a simple average of the ages of all domestic buildings in the development measured in years. Development scale (SCL) was denoted by the total number of residential units within a MOH development. The coordination mechanism of housing management for a development (COM) was assessed based on whether an owners' corporation has been formed or not within the development. The variable was equal to 1 if the MOH development had an owners' corporation and zero if otherwise.

Lastly, perceived neighbor relationship (NREL) was gauged with a single-item scale. A resident was asked to rate the neighbor relationship in his or her housing development using a five-point scale (5 = very good; 4 = good; 3 = neither good nor poor; 2 = poor; 1 = very poor). Very often, single-item indicators are regarded as less valid and less reliable. However, we did not think that there would be any reliability and validity issues for this measurement item. The question is very straightforward so no interpretation concern is envisaged. The better was the neighbor relationship perceived by a resident, the higher would be the rating given for the variable. Similar to residential satisfaction, an aggregated level of perceived neighbor relationship for a MOH development was obtained by taking a simple average of all individual neighbor relationship scores.

4.2 Sampling of MOH developments and data collection

Primary and secondary data were collected in Sham Shui Po and Tsuen Wan, Hong Kong in 2016 and 2017. These two districts were chosen because they accommodated a large number of MOH developments with a wide variety, ranging from old medium-rise standalone buildings to newly-built high-rise estate-type developments. Since the most precise level of official census data publicly released in Hong Kong was the street-block level, we targeted only medium- and large-scale MOH developments for our empirical study. If small-scale housing developments were included in the research, the socio-demographic data obtained from the census could not be mapped exactly with the development-specific data as a street-block contained domestic buildings belonging to different developments. Random sampling is adopted to achieve a representative and useful sample. First, a roster of MOH developments with at least 350 domestic units was compiled. Then, 350 MOH developments were then randomly selected. An invitation letter was sent to the PMA or homeowner association of each of these selected developments to participate in the research. Finally, 217 invitees, or 62.0% of the invited MOH developments, agreed to partake in the research.

The processes of data collection are portrayed in **Figure 2**. First, basic information of the MOH developments was obtained in a desk study in which record building plans were studied and data were retrieved from various government databases (e.g. building management database [49] and 2016 Population By-census dataset). This stage aimed to gather development-based information such as development scales, building ages and resident socio-demographic profiles. In the second stage, site visits were conducted for assessing the actual building conditions of the MOH developments under investigation. In the third stage, a resident survey was conducted. Not less than 5% of the domestic units in each of the 217 housing developments under investigation were randomly sampled. The householders of these units were invited to complete a structured questionnaire online. The questionnaire included questions regarding respondents' perceived levels of residential satisfaction and neighbor relationship, and perceived quality of the PMA's service. The questionnaire was pretested and fine-tuned before official start of the survey. A total of 9000 invitations were sent out and 1649 complete replies were received, representing a response rate of 18.3%.

Table 1 summarizes the characteristics of the 217 MOH developments under investigation. The mean age of the MOH developments was 23.4. These developments had quite diverse scales, ranging from 353 to 6324 domestic units. Similarly, education and income profiles of the MOH developments varied a lot. The

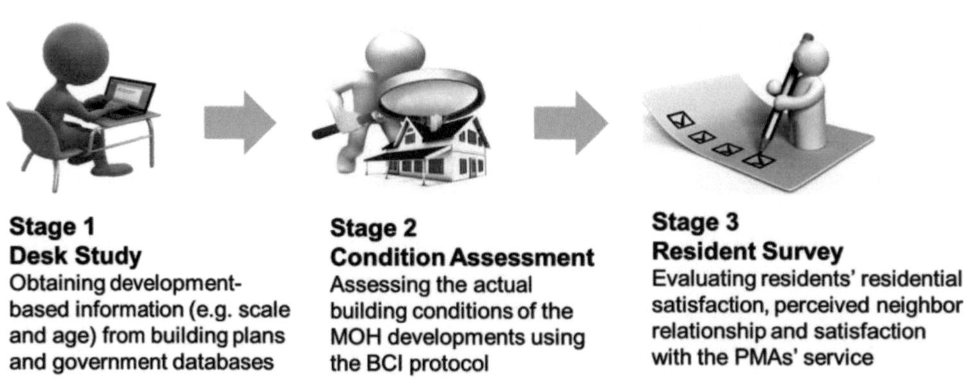

Figure 2.
Processes of data collection for the empirical study.

DOI: http://dx.doi.org/10.5772/intechopen.81166

	Maximum	Mean	Minimum	σ
Age (years)	48	23.4	2	9.9
Number of domestic units (no.)	6324	956.4	353	1352.7
Percentage of owner-occupiers (%)	99.2	78.5	58.4	9.7
Median monthly domestic household income (HK$)	75,980	41,305.9	13,700	16,081.1
Percentage of population aged 15 and over attaining post-secondary education level (%)	62.9	42.1	17.1	11.6
Median age of population(years)	48.0	39.4	27.9	4.3

Table 1.
Characteristics of the 217MOH developments included in the final analysis.

	Maximum	Mean	Minimum	σ
BCI	95.7	62.1	30.2	18.1
Residential Satisfaction	4.1	3.2	2.2	0.4

Table 2.
BCI and residential satisfaction scores of the 217 MOH developments.

percentage of population aged 15 and over attaining post-secondary education level ranged from 17.1 to 62.9%, with a standard deviation of 11.6%. The median monthly domestic household income ranged from HK$13,700 to HK$75,980, with a standard deviation of HK$16,081.1. On average, 78.5% of the households in each of these housing developments owner-occupied their domestic units. The average median age of population was 39.4. 124 out of 217 developments (57.1%) have an owners' corporation. **Table 2** tabulates the summary statistics of the BCI and residential satisfaction scores of the 217 developments.

4.3 Findings

For simplicity, the functions in Eqs. (1) and (2) are expressed in linear form such that

$$PC = \alpha_0 + \alpha_1 RAGE + \alpha_2 INC + \alpha_3 EDU + \alpha_4 DAGE + \alpha_5 SCL + \alpha_6 COM + \varepsilon \quad (4)$$

and

$$RS = \beta_0 + \beta_1 RAGE + \beta_2 INC + \beta_3 EDU + \beta_4 TEN + \beta_5 NREL + \gamma \quad (5)$$

where α_i (for $i = 0, 1, 2, \ldots, 6$) and β_j (for $j = 0, 1, 2, \ldots, 5$) are coefficients to be estimated. Eqs. (4) and (5) were estimated using the ordinary least square (OLS) technique with the development-based data of the 217 MOH developments. Before model estimation, all continuous variables, including both dependent and independent variables, were rescaled to the range [0, 1] so the error series of the two estimated models can be integrated in a meaningful manner. The results of the OLS estimation were shown in **Table 3**. Generally speaking, the two models had very high explanatory power as demonstrated by the high adjusted-R^2 values. From the estimation results of Model (1), RAGE, EDU and DAGE were found to be significant determinants of PC. On the other hand, the estimation results of Model (2) indicate that INC and TEN were the only two variables with significant impacts on RS.

Variable	Model (1)		Model (2)	
	Coefficient	t-statistic	Coefficient	t-statistic
Constant	1.0361***	21.2868	0.8139***	20.8062
RAGE	−0.1160**	−2.0976	0.0674	1.4964
INC	−0.0052	−0.1595	−0.4690***	−18.4349
EDU	0.1073 *	1.7103	0.0018	0.0376
DAGE	−0.7754 ***	−28.7315	—	—
SCL	1.0361	−0.2112	—	—
COM	−0.1160	1.6763	—	—
TEN	—	—	0.0011*	−2.6407
NREL	—	—	0.8139	0.1297
Dependent Variable	PC		RS	
R2	0.9030		0.8360	
Adjusted *R2*	0.9002		0.8321	
F-statistic	325.7408 ***		215.0589 ***	

*Notes: *** denotes p < 0.01; ** denotes p < 0.05; and * denotes p < 0.1.*

Table 3.
Results of the OLS estimation.

	Maximum	Mean	Minimum	σ
ε	0.1822	0	−0.1577	0.0563
γ	0.0981	0	−0.1235	0.0446
PMPI	0.2089	0	−0.2801	0.0695

Table 4.
Descriptive statistics of the PMPI and its components.

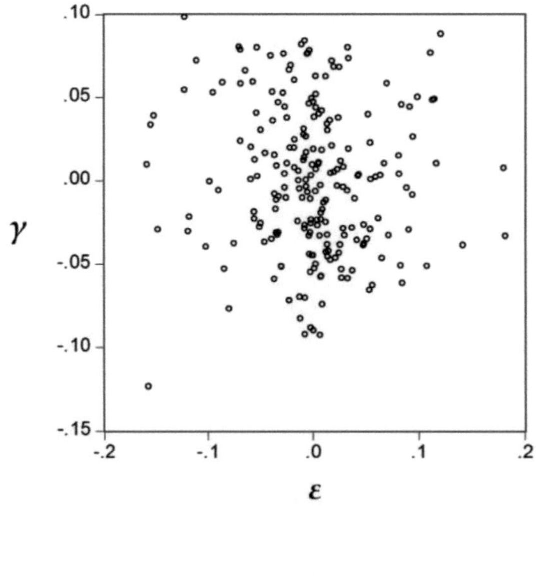

Figure 3.
Scatter plot of ε and γ.

The residual series of the two estimated models were then extracted and the PMPI scores of the 217 MOH developments were computed accordingly. As illustrated in **Table 4**, the highest PMPI score was 0.2089 and the lowest was −0.2801. **Figure 3** shows the scatter plot of ε and γ. As a whole, while 107 PMAs (49.3%) received a positive PMPI score, only 50 PMAs got positive values for both ε and γ.

5. Validation of the PMPI framework and discussion

5.1 Validation of the framework

At this point, one may argue that the performance of a PMA in the management of a MOH development can be evaluated based on the opinions of the residents in the development. Many previous studies on the quality of property management or facility management service adopted the subjective approach [50–55]. Yet, the reliability of the subjective quality service measures is often undermined by evaluators' biases and sensitive to evaluators' expectations and previous experiences [56, 57]. Nonetheless, such subjective assessment of PMA's performance can be a good candidate for validating the proposed PMPI. It is believed that the PMPI for a PMA managing a particular MOH development should have an unambiguous positive relationship with the PMA's service quality perceived by the clients, i.e. the residents, in the development.

We adopted the SERVQUAL model to evaluate a PMA's service quality because it has been widely used in the property management and facility management industries [50, 58, 59]. Based on the SERVQUAL model, five dimensions of a PMA's service quality were evaluated. As shown in **Table 5**, these five dimensions were further broken down into 19 statements or items for operationalization [60–62]. Residents were asked to rate their levels of agreement with the each statements using a five-point scale (with 1 = strongly disagree and 5 = strongly agree). For each resident, the overall SERVQUAL is taken as a simple average of the scores for the 19 items. An aggregate SERVQUAL score was calculated for each MOH development by taking a simple average of all individual residents' overall SERVQUAL scores.

To validate the PMPI, Pearson's correlation test was performed based on the 217 pairs of PMPI and SERVQUAL scores. A correlation coefficient of 0.84 ($p < 0.01$) was returned, signifying that there is an unambiguous strong positive relationship between the PMPI and SERVQUAL scores. Such findings confirmed the validity of the proposed PMPI framework.

5.2 Discussion

Professional property management is crucial for the long-term sustainability of housing assets, particularly the MOH developments. For various reasons like agency problems, PMAs need not necessarily perform well when managing a MOH development. To realize strategic management of housing stock in Hong Kong, we need to apprehend how the PMA perform. While different performance measures have been proposed in the literature, they have different limitations. Actually, the performance of PMAs in MOH management remains largely unobserved or incomparable in practice. The PMPI framework proposed and validated in the chapter aims to fill up the extant research gap by offering a tool for evaluating a PMA's performance in a *ceteris paribus* condition. From the perspective of knowledge contribution, the current study advances the research frontier of strategic management to the arena of property management. Besides, there are several practical implications of this

Dimension	Items
Tangibles	• Your PMA has modern equipment and tools for housing management. • The physical facilities in your housing development are properly maintained. • Employees of your PMA are neat-appearing.
Reliability	• Employees of your PMA tell you exactly when the service is performed. • When your PMA promises to do something by a certain time, they will do so. • When you have a problem, your PMA will show a sincere interest in solving it. • Your PMA performs the service right the first time.
Responsiveness	• Employees of your PMA give prompt service to you. • Employees of your PMA are always willing to help you. • Employees of your PMA are never too busy to respond to your requests.
Assurance	• The behavior of employers of your PMA instills confidence in you. • You feel safe in your housing development. • Employees of your PMA are consistently courteous with you. • Employees of your PMA have the knowledge to manage your housing development.
Empathy	• Your PMA will give you enough attention. • Your PMA has operating hours convenient to you. • Your PMA have employees who give your personal attention. • Your PMA have your best interests at heart. • Employees of your PMA understand your specific needs.

Table 5.
The SERVQUAL scale adopted for validation of PMPI.

research which can induce the cultivation of a culture of quality MOH management in Hong Kong in the long run.

First, the PMPI framework allows the extraction of hidden property management performance from a number of observable or measurable variables. For homeowners or residents, the PMPI provides a useful tool for benchmarking PMAs with regard to their property management performance. The index serves to inform people on the relative performance of the PMAs. For instance, homeowners, potential buyers, and potential tenants can refer to the PMPI to decide whether or not to make a property transaction or rent a property. It is of paramount importance to these parties because PMAs play vital roles in shaping the quality of the living environment which in turn determines residents' life quality and property values.

Second, the PMPI framework enables an objective inter-PMA comparison for distinguishing the good from the bad. It is believed that a well-publicized and well-received PMPI can serve as a benchmarking tool to measure and compare PMAs' performance in MOH management. Such performance benchmarking can introduce competition in the property management sector. The PMPI informs the PMAs of their performance relative to their competitors. In order to get a higher PMPI score, they need to continuously monitor and improve their services. Under-performing

PMAs, as identified by the low PMPI scores, will be punished by the market as no one is willing to appoint them for managing properties.

Third, PMPI contains important information, which assists property management companies to make more sensible decisions in resource allocation. Sizeable property management companies usually manage a large portfolio of MOH developments with different teams. The PMPI can be used to compare the performance of different teams. Resources from the head office can be directed to the most needy teams (i.e. teams with lowest PMPI scores), say by providing more staff training or conducting more frequent performance audits. Fourth, the PMPI can serve as a policy tool to identify substandard management service providers. The licensing authority can make reference to a PMA's PMPI when making decisions regarding licensing and disciplinary actions.

This study demonstrates how PMAs' performance is measured and benchmarked in a novel way. In fact, its findings can be associated with other principles of strategic management. For example, in order to stay ahead of the curve, a PMA should either do something in achieving better building condition or a higher level of residential satisfaction. The PMA should think about what goals it should aim at to establish sustainable competitive advantages over its competitors [63]. It may need to offer different services than its competitors or deliver similar services in different ways [64]. Strategic management concerns with adaptation of an organization's internal environment to the changing external business environment or contexts [65]. In this light, PMAs should observe and proactively respond to the changes in the external business environment such as advancement in information and communication technology (ICT) and law revisions. Further studies should be carried out to investigate if PMAs that are more responsive to these external changes (e.g. by earlier application of ICT in the property management processes) will perform better.

6. Conclusion

"Best of the class" today may not stay on the top of the league tomorrow [66]. Therefore, continual improvement in service quality is needed in the world of changes. Property management is no exception to this rule. In many high-rise cities, homeowners and residents engage an external PMA in the management of their MOH developments with the expectation to ensure the living environment is healthy, safe and pleasant. Nonetheless, as a profit-making entity, the PMA do not often share the goals and interests with its client. Agency problems are natural results in MOH management in many cases, leading to poor management performance and bringing about negative social, economic, and environmental implications. To cope with the existing challenges, evaluation and benchmarking of performance of PMAs are becoming essential. On one hand, these help homeowners and residents to make more informed decisions in PMA selection. On the other hand, competition is introduced through benchmarking so better services provided by PMAs can be promoted. Nonetheless, extant indicators and measures of PMA performance have different limitations. In this regard, a new paradigm for evaluation of PMA performance in management of MOH developments in Hong Kong was proposed.

The PMPI developed in this chapter have multiple applications which can make valuable contributions to the property management field. From the practical perspective, the PMPI facilitates performance benchmarking given that when a critical mass of PMAs have been evaluated using the index. The index serves as a tool for informing the general public about the management performance of PMAs in MOH management. In the procurement of management service and service contract renewal, homeowners can make reference to the performance indices of different PMAs for better decision making. For the PMAs themselves, the framework allows the PMAs to know their relative positions in the performance league so they can continuously monitor and improve their services. In the medium to long run, under-performing PMAs will be identified by the PMPI and crowded out from the market. This is promising for a culture of quality property or MOH management to foster in Hong Kong.

On the academic side, with the PMPI, research opportunities to explore the determinants of PMA performance in the future are opened up. Researchers can identify what kinds of contractual arrangement lead to better performance of PMA. Furthermore, the relationship between property price or rent and PMPI can be tested. From the viewpoint of economics, properties managed by a better-performing PMA should command higher values or rents than those managed by a poorly-performing PMA. In this regard, the PMPI can further be validated with property value or rent. The average property price or rent of a MOH development is expected to change positively with the PMPI of the PMA managing the development, keeping other things constant.

Acknowledgements

The final form of this chapter owes much to the discussion at the 2nd International Conference on Social Science and Development held in Chengdu on 28-29 May 2016 and the 22nd Annual Conference of the Asian Real Estate Society held in Taichung on 9-11 July 2017 [67, 68]. The work described in this chapter was fully supported by a grant from the Research Grants Council of the Hong Kong Special Administrative Region, China [Project No. CityU 17201215].

Conflict of interest

The authors declare that there is no conflict of interest.

Author details

Yung Yau[1*] and Daniel Chi Wing Ho[2]

1 Department of Public Policy, City University of Hong Kong, Hong Kong, China

2 Faculty of Design and Environment, Technological and Higher Education Institute of Hong Kong, Hong Kong, China

*Address all correspondence to: y.yau@cityu.edu.hk

References

[1] Porter M. Competitive Strategy: Techniques for Analyzing Industries and Competitors. New York: Free Press; 1980. 369 p

[2] Lawrence P, Lorsch J. Differentiation and integration in complex organizations. Administrative Science Quarterly. 1967;**12**:1-47. DOI: 10.2307/2391211

[3] Miles R, Snow C. Organizational Strategy, Structure, and Process. Stanford: Stanford University Press; 2003. 304 p

[4] Andrews K. The concept of corporate strategy. In: Foss N, editor. Resources, Firms, and Strategies: A Reader in the Resource-Based Perspective. Oxford: Oxford University Press; 1997. pp. 52-59

[5] Mintzberg H. Patterns in strategy formation. Management Science. 1978;**24**:934-948. DOI: 10.1287/mnsc.24.9.934

[6] Huff A, Reger R. A review of strategic process research. Journal of Management. 1987;**13**:211-236. DOI: 10.1177/014920638701300203

[7] Langley A. Strategies for theorizing from process data. Academy of Management Review. 1999;**24**:691-710. DOI: 10.5465/amr.1999.2553248

[8] Jasper M. What is strategic management. Journal of Nursing Management. 2012;**20**:838-846. DOI: 10.111/jonm.12001

[9] Wong S, Tang B, van Horen B. Strategic urban management in China: A case study of Guangzhou Development District. Habitat International. 2006;**30**:645-667. DOI: 10.1016/j.habitatint.2005.04.001

[10] Page S, Hardyman R. Place marketing and town Centre management: A new tool for urban revitalization. Cities. 1996;**13**:153-164. DOI: 10.1016/0264-2751(96)00002-9

[11] Yau Y. Perceived efficacies and collectivism in multi-owned housing management. Habitat International. 2014;**43**:133-141. DOI: 10.1016/j.habitatint.2014.02.009

[12] Hastings E, Wong S, Walters M. Governance in a co-ownership environment: The management of multi-ownership property in Hong Kong. Property Management. 2006;**24**:293-308. DOI: 10.1108/02637470610660165

[13] Loo K. A Guide to Effective Property Management in Hong Kong. Hong Kong: Hong Kong University Press; 1991. 185 p

[14] Ho D, Yau Y, Wong S, Cheung A, Chau K, Leung H. Effects of building management regimes of private apartment buildings in Hong Kong. Property Management. 2006;**24**:309-321. DOI: 10.1108/02637470610660174

[15] Yau Y, Ho D, Chau K. Determinants of the safety performance of private multi-storey residential buildings in Hong Kong. Social Indicators Research. 2008;**89**:501-521. DOI: 10.1007/s11205-008-9246-3

[16] Yiu C. Building depreciation and sustainable development. Journal of Building Appraisal. 2007;**3**:97-103. DOI: 10.1057/palgrave.jba.2950072

[17] Yau Y. The value of building safety: A hedonic price approach. Urbani izziv. 2015;**26**:92-104. DOI: 10.5379/urbani-izziv-en-2015-26-01-003

[18] Yau Y, Lau W, Ho D. Principle of selectivity in housing rehabilitation subsidies: Case study in Hong Kong. Journal of Urban Planning and Development. 2015;**141**:1-10. DOI: 10.1061/(ASCE)UP.1943-5444.0000231

[19] Hui E. Key success factors of building management in large and dense residential estates. Facilities. 2005;**23**: 47-62. DOI: 10.1108/02632770510575893

[20] Chen S, Webster C. Homeowners associations, collective action and the costs of private governance. Housing Studies. 2005;**20**:205-220. DOI: 10.1080/0267303042000331736

[21] Yiu C, Wong S, Yau Y. Property management as property rights governance: Exclusion and internal conflict resolution. Property Management. 2006;**24**:87-97. DOI: 10.1108/02637470610657989

[22] Kyle R. Property Management. 7th ed. Chicago: Dearborn Real Estate Education; 2005. 530 p

[23] Davis J, Schoorman D, Donaldson L. Towards a stewardship theory of management. Academy of Management Review. 1997;**22**:20-47. DOI: DOI 10.5465/amr.1997.9707180258

[24] Dalton D, Hitt M, Certo S, Dalton C. The fundamental agency problem and its mitigation. The Academy of Management Annals. 2007;**1**:1-64. DOI: 10.1080/078559806

[25] Bonazzi L, Islam S. Agency theory and corporate governance: A study of the effectiveness of board in their monitoring of the CEO. Journal of Modelling in Management. 2007;**2**:7-23. DOI: 10.1108/17465660710733022

[26] Guilding C, Warnken J, Ardill A, Fredline L. An agency theory perspective on the owner/manager relationship in tourism-based condominiums. Tourism Management. 2005;**26**:409-420. DOI: 10.1016/j.tourman.2003.11.021

[27] Rosenberg S, Corgel J. Agency costs in apartment property management contracts. Real Estate Economics. 1990;**18**:184-201. DOI: 10.1111/1540-6229.00516

[28] Yip N, Chang C, Hung T. Modes of condominium management: A principal-agent perspective. Facilities. 2007;**25**:215-226. DOI: 10.1108/02632770710742183

[29] Thomson J. Strata Schemes in NSW Accused of Employing 'Slave Labour' [Internet]. 2016. Available from: https://www.domain.com.au/news/strata-schemes-in-nsw-accused-of-employing-slave-labour-20160530-gp79yn/ [Accessed: 2018-05-30]

[30] Domain. CSI: Corrupt Strata Investigations [Internet]. 2011. Available from https://www.domain.com.au/news/csi-corrupt-strata-investigations-20111202-1o9nd/ [Accessed: 2018-05-30]

[31] The Standard. Ex-Manager Charged with Bribery over Garden Vista Renovations [Internet]. 2018. Available from http://www.thestandard.com.hk/breaking-news.php?id=104629 [Accessed: 2018-05-30]

[32] Landlords. Former ACC Property Manager Pleads Guilty to Corruption Charges. 2011. Available from https://www.landlords.co.nz/article/3905/former-acc-property-manager-pleads-guilty-to-corruption-charges [Accessed: 2018-05-30]

[33] All Property Management. Property Management Laws by State [Internet]. Available from https://www.allpropertymanagement.com/propertylaw [Accessed: 2018-05-30]

[34] Harbour Times. New Property Management Services Licensing Regime Passes Key LegCo Hurdle [Internet]. Available from http://harbourtimes.com/2016/05/27/new-property-management-services-licensing-regime-passes-key-legco-hurdle/ [Accessed: 2018-05-30]

[35] Prašnikar J, Debeljak Ž, Ahčan A. Benchmarking as a tool

of strategic management. Total Quality Management and Business Excellence. 2005;**16**:257-275. DOI: 10.1080/14783360500054400

[36] Kemp P. Researching housing management performance. Urban Studies. 1995;**32**:779-790. DOI: 10.1080/00420989550012889

[37] Chen W, Jian J, Chen H. Apartment building management performance assessment using data envelopment analysis. In: Proceedings of the 2015 International Conference on Operations Excellence and Service Engineering; 10-11 September 2015; Orlando. Michigan: IEOM Society; 2015. pp. 110-116

[38] Lam T. Optimisation of performance management for housing services. Journal of Facilities Management. 2008;**6**:226-240. DOI: 10.1108/14725960810890154

[39] Hinton M, Francis G, Holloway J. Best practice benchmarking in the UK. Benchmarking. An International Journal. 2000;**7**:52-61. DOI: 10.1108/14635770010314954

[40] Hui E, Lau H, Khan T. Effect of property management on property price: A case study in HK. Facilities. 2011;**29**:459-471. DOI: 10.1108/02632771111157132

[41] Chin L, Poh L. Implementing quality in property management: The case of Singapore. Property Management. 1999;**17**:310-320. DOI: 10.1108/02637479910299624

[42] Lee T. The development of ISO 9000 certification and the future of quality management: A survey of certified firms in Hong Kong. International Journal of Quality and Reliability Management. 1998;**15**:162-177. DOI: 10.1108/02656719810204766

[43] Yau Y, Ho D. The effects of building management practices on residential property prices in Hong Kong. Journal of Building Appraisal. 2009;**4**:157-168. DOI: 10.1057/jba.2008.42

[44] Kuo C, Lin C, Chen C. Developing performance indicators for residential service. Journal of Property Management. 2011;**2**:65-74

[45] Pan N, Liu C. Property management performance evaluation system. Journal of Property Management. 2010;**1**:1-14

[46] Sharpe W. Asset allocation: Management style and performance measurement. Journal of Portfolio Management. 1992;**18**:7-19. DOI: 10.3905/jpm.1992.409394

[47] Yau Y. Building conditions in Yau Tsim Mong, Hong Kong: Appraisal, exploration and estimation. Journal of Building Appraisal. 2008;**3**:319-329. DOI: 10.1057/jba.2008.8

[48] Rent G, Rent C. Low-income housing: Factors related to residential satisfaction. Environment and Behavior. 1978;**10**:459-488. DOI: 10.1177/001391657801000401

[49] Home Affairs Department. Database of private buildings in Hong Kong. 2018. Available from https://bmis1.buildingmgt.gov.hk/ [Accessed: 2018-05-30]

[50] Yusoff W, Ismail M, Newell G. FM-SERVQUAL: A new approach of service quality measurement framework in local authorities. Journal of Corporate Real Estate. 2008;**10**:130-144. DOI: 10.1108/14630010810905633

[51] Baharum Z, Nawai A, Saat Z. Assessment of property management service quality of purpose built office buildings. International Business Research. 2009;**2**:162-174. DOI: 10.5539/ibr.v2n1p162

[52] Shaw D, Haynes B. An evaluation of customer perception of FM service

delivery. Facilities. 2004;**22**:170-177. DOI: 10.1108/02632770410547534

[53] Hui E, Zheng X. Measuring customer satisfaction of FM service in housing sector: A structural equation model approach. Facilities. 2010;**28**:306-320. DOI: 10.1108/02632771011031538

[54] Tuch M, Smith A. User perceptions in workplace productivity and strategic FM delivery. Facilities. 2008;**26**:163-178. DOI: 10.1108/02632770810864989

[55] Li L, Siu A. Privatising management services in subsidised housing in Hong Kong. Property Management. 2001;**19**:37-49. DOI: 10.1108/02637470110366194

[56] Eboli L, Mazzulla G. A methodology for evaluating transit service quality based on subjective and objective measures from the passenger's point of view. Transport Policy. 2011;**18**:172-181. DOI: 10.1016/j.tranpol.2010.07.007

[57] Cronin J, Taylor S. SERVPERF versus SERVQUAL: Reconciling performance-based and perceptions-minus-expectations measurement of service quality. Journal of Marketing. 1994;**58**:125-131. DOI: 10.2307/1252256

[58] Chan C, Ng Y, Casimir G. Confucian dynamism, affective commitment, need for achievement, and service quality: A study on property managers in Hong Kong. Services Marketing Quarterly. 2011;**32**:318-331. DOI: 10.1080/15332969.2011.606763

[59] Mohammad M, Gambo Y, Omirin M. Assessing facilities management service in postgraduate hostel using Servqual technique. Journal of Emerging Trends in Economics and Management Sciences. 2012;**3**:485-490

[60] Hoxley M. The fee tendering and service quality issue revisited. Property Management. 2007;**25**:180-192. DOI: 10.1108/02637470710741533

[61] Parasuraman A, Zeithaml V, Berry L. SERVQUAL: A multiple-item scale for measuring consumer perceptions of service quality. Journal of Retailing. 1988;**64**:12-40

[62] Parasuraman A, Zeithaml V, Berry L. Refinement and reassessment of the SERVQUAL scale. Journal of Retailing. 1991;**67**:420-450

[63] Porter M. Strategy and the internet. Harvard Business Review. 2001;**79**:63-78

[64] Chew E, Gottschalk P. Information Technology Strategy and Management. Hershey: Information Science Reference; 2009. 496 p

[65] Panfil G, Nechita D. Fundamental principles in strategic management. European Journal of Public Order and National Security. 2015;**8**:5-10

[66] Kouzmin A, Löffler E, Klages H, Korac-Kakabadse N. Benchmarking and performance measurement in public sectors: Towards learning for agency effectiveness. International Journal of Public Sector Management. 1999;**12**:121-144. DOI: 10.1108/09513559910263462

[67] Yau Y, Ho D. A new paradigm for evaluating performance of property management agents. In: Proceedings of the 2nd International Conference on Social Science and Development; 28-29 May 2016; Chengdu. Lancaster: DEStech; 2016. pp. 188-193

[68] Yau Y, Ho D. Evaluation of property management agent performance: A novel empirical model. In: Presented at the 22nd Annual Conference of the Asian Real Estate Society; 9-11 July 2017; Taichung

Chapter 5

Organizational Identity, Corporate Strategy, and Habits of Attention: A Case Study of Toyota

Charles McMillan

Abstract

This chapter links organizational identity as a cohesive attribute to corporate strategy and a competitive advantage, using Toyota as a case study. The evolution of Toyota from a domestic producer, and exporter, and now a global firm using a novel form of lean production follows innovative tools of human resources, supply chain collaboration, a network identity to link domestic operations to overseas investments, and unparalleled commercial investments in technologies that make the firm moving from a sustainable competitive position to one of unassailable advantage in the global auto sector. The chapter traces the strategic moves to strength Toyota's identity at all levels, including in its overseas operations, to build a global ecosystem model of collaboration.

Keywords: institutional identity, lean management, learning symmetries, docility, habits of attention, kaizen

(Article for Lawrence Emeagwali (Ed.), Strategic Management. London, 2018)

October 18, 2018.

"There is no use trying" said Alice, "we cannot believe impossible things."—Lewis Carroll

1. Introduction

Few organizations combine the institutional benefits of longevity and tradition with the disruptive startup advantages of novelty and suspension of path dependent behavior. This chapter provides a case study of Toyota Corporation, an organization with an explicit philosophy that embodies "...standardized work and kaizen (that) are two sides of the same coin. Standardized work provides a consistent basis for maintaining productivity, quality and safety at high levels. Kaizen furnishes the dynamics of continuing improvement and the very human motivation of encouraging individuals to take part in designing and managing their own jobs" ([1], p. 38). Toyota's philosophy, combining a model that is "stable and paranoid, systematic experimental, formal and frank" [2], often called the Toyota Way, evolved from the founding of Toyoda Automatic Loom Works, founded in 1911, setting up an auto division in 1933, and Toyota Motor Company in 1937 [3].

What is unique about Toyota and its pioneering lean production, described colloquially as just-in-time (JIT), embraces a deliberative philosophy that establishes a corporate identity for safety, quality, and aspirational performance goals. Going forward, with plants and distribution centers around the world, Toyota cultivates a direct involvement of employees, suppliers, and other organizations, called the Toyota Group, as a network identity that extends boundary members of the firm's eco-system that also embodies detailed performance measures to strengthen and reinforce identity enhancement. These identity attributes creating novel and seemingly contradictory configurations, both at home and now in global markets. Toyota provides a framework to link identity as a cohesive attribute for problem-solving with explicit, data-driven benchmarks, a DNA that encompasses observation, analysis, hypothesis testing from the shop floor to the executive suite [3, 4].

The concept of *identity* has a long pedigree in the social sciences, dating from classical writers like Adam Smith, Karl Marx, Max Weber, and Emile Durkheim, focusing on individual identities separate and distinct from larger social systems arising from the division of labor. However, identity in organizations is a relatively new construct, based on claims that are "central, distinctive, and enduring" [5]. Despite the growing literature on organizational identity [6, 7], there is less consensus given the multiple disciplinary focus, the levels of analysis, well as minimum empirical work linking organizational identity to corporate strategy. In some cases, identity linkages touch on outcomes like brand equity, reputation, visual media like social networking and the gap between defining what the organization is today and what it wants to become, despite the high failure rate of firms [8]. Indeed, there is little reason to doubt that "the concept of organizational identity is suffering an identity crisis" ([9], p. 206).

Despite the growing literature on organization identity, encompassing diverse constructs and methodologies [6, 7], often at different organizational levels (individuals, groups and senior management), has limited empirical study linking individual and group identity both to corporate strategy and corporate performance. Various accounts of social experiences, concentrating on a sense of insider and outsider to frame a mutual identity mindset that shapes organizational identity, apply personal histories and narratives, but leave open the distinction between corporate identity and organizational identity [10]. Identity producing mechanisms flowing from purposeful actions vary by context, such as universities and faith-based organizations to technology and engineering organizations with complicated role activities grounded in socio-technical design [11]. Compelling cases of identity as a tool for organizational integration, or the impact of cleavage and conflict owing to human diversity policies, personality characteristics of key actors, and sub-unit identity images advance understanding of behavior within organizations, but often ignores how both strategic choice and external forces impact these internal mindsets. Many scholars associate internal identity issues to external stakeholders using sundry communication tools (e.g., [12]) but the literature has few studies that explain what organizational identity features are truly different and give a competitive advantage in contested markets over time. To advance hypothesis testing and to encourage conceptual development in both theory and practice, there must be a linkage to identity as a construct that provides insights to an organization's competitive advantage.

This chapter addresses the issues linking strategic choices and capabilities to Toyota's identity as a case study. Toyota's strategic positioning and high-performance outcomes amplify identity tools at three levels, its employees (both in Japan and its factories overseas), its suppliers, and its customers. Depicted as a best practice company [13], Toyota is seen as a model to emulate in sectors as diverse as hospitals and retailing. This chapter has three objectives: first, by examining Toyota's transformation as a leading domestic producer to a top global company, the firm's core identity has changed little despite numerous internal and external changes; second, Toyota as a case study illustrates the capacity to have multiple images in different contexts, without sacrificing its core identity; and third, the chapter offers recommendations for empirical studies of organizational identity.

2. Organizational identification and identity

In their seminal article, Stuart and Whetten [5] put forward the concept of organizational identity constituting a set of "claims" and specified what was central, distinctive and enduring, but recognizing that organizations can have multiple identities and claims that can be contradictory, ambiguous, or even unrelated. While some authors have attempted to provide more clarity, Pratt addresses the construct of identity and its generality, stating it was "often overused and under specified" beyond general statements about "who are we?" and "who do we want to become?"

Historically, identity and identification are described in classical writings focusing on societies, social systems, and their constituent parts. Such examples as Adam Smith in economics on the division of labor, Babbage on the division of work tasks, Marx on division of social class, Max Weber on the division of status and occupation, and Durkheim on differentiated social structures, each contributed to current views of how individuals, groups, and teams become a cohesive collective in a complex organization. More specifically, Durkheim's [14] analysis of the division of labor and differentiated social structures with distinct socio-psychological values and impacts required variations in role homogeneity in sub-systems.[1] His views influenced subsequent writers as diverse as Freud in psychiatry and Harold Laswell in political theory, whose study of world politics includes a chapter entitled "Nations and Classes: The Symbols of Identification."

Simon [15] introduced identification to organization theory, describing it as follows: "the process of identification permits the broad organizational arrangements to govern the decisions of the persons who participate in the structure" (p. 102). More specifically, "a person identifies himself with a group when, in making a decision, he evaluates the several alternatives of choice in terms of their consequences for the specified group" in contrast to personal motivation, where "his evaluation is based upon an identification with himself or his family" ([16], p. 206). Both the fault lines of identity, based on status, perverse incentives, class or occupation, as well as group identification [17] impact organizational performance by variations in shared goals and preferences, as well as forms of interaction and feedback, often enhanced or lessoned by recruitment patterns and work rules and incentives.

Identity and identification as reference points in organizations also flow from the configuration of roles, role structures, and "clusters of activities" where "a person has an occupational self-identity and is motivated to behave in ways which affirm and enhance the value attributes of that identity" ([18], p. 179). Theories of social identity assume individual identity is partitioned into ingroups and outgroups is social situations and organizational life, often with an implicit cost–benefit calculation, but acts of altruistic behavior, where behavioral norms benefit the welfare of others, often seen in "collectivist societies," strengthens organizational identity [19]. Other approaches take a social constructionist approach,

[1] To quote Durkeim [14] directly, "...as we advance in the evolutionary scale, the ties which bind the individual to his family, to his native soil, to traditions which the past has given to him, to collective group images, become loose...' (p. 259).

emphasizing social and cultural perspectives [20], where sense-making comes from stories and narratives of everyday experience [21], thereby, "...in linking identity and narrative in an individual, we link an individual [career] story to a particular cultural and historical narrative of a group" [22]. Going further, Dutton et al. [23] speculate that organizational identification is a process of self-categorization cultivated by distinctive, central, and enduring attributes that get reflected in corporate image, reputation, or strategic vision. Alvesson [24] describes the need for identity alignment: "...by strengthening the organization's identity—its experienced distinctiveness, consistency, and stability—it can be assumed that individual identities and identification will be strengthen with what they are supposed to be doing at their work place."

While some studies [25] purport to focus on managerial strategies that project images as a tool to shape distinctive identities with stakeholders, the reality is that organizational identities without corresponding integration of individual, sub-unit, or group identification may lead to behavioral frictions, and detachment via lower compliance and cues of detachment. Conflict and cleavages affect group-binding identification, often persisting as conformity of opinion, forms of social interaction, and group loyalties, as well as enhancing internal legitimacy for desired outcomes. While both individuals and groups may have multiple and loosely connected identities, there remains lingering organizations dysfunctions that exacerbate cleavage and conflict, such as hypocrisy, selective amnesia, or disloyalty [18]. Psychological exit comes from unsatisfactory outcomes, a form of weakening organizational identity and strengthening group identity to give voice for remedial actions [26]. In the extreme, such sub-identities found in groups and sub-units compete with other forms of identification and may lead to organizational dysfunctions [17].

Akerlof and Kranton [27] view organizational identity, with emphasis on why firms must transform workers from outsiders to insiders, as a form of motivational capital. In short, a distinctive identity is a distinctive competence. To quote Likert [28]. "the favorable attitudes towards the organization and the work are not those of easy complacency but are the attitudes of identification with the organization and its objectives and a high sense of involvement in achieving them" (p. 98). Other theorists suggest variations in organizational identity impact sense-making and interpretative processes [29], internalization of learning [10] and processes linking shared values and modes of performance [30].

Identity and identification cues, viewed as the mental perceptions of individual self-awareness, social interactions and experiences, and self-esteem have many antecedents, such as social class [31], demographic factors like age, race, religion, or sex [32], and national culture and identity [33]. Studies emphasizing social construction perspectives stem from individual accounts, often defined in social narratives, histories, and biographies rooted in time and place [34]. As Hammack [22] emphasizes, "...in linking identity and narrative in an individual, we link an individual story to a particular cultural and historical narrative of a group" (p. 230). At a general level, organizational culture depicts the set of norms and values that are widely shared and strongly held throughout the organization [35], and refers to the "unspoken code of communication among members of an organization" [36] and aids and supplements task coordination and group identity. In this way, individual employees better understand the premises of decision choices in problem solving at the organizational level. In complex organizations, identity is linked to the strategic capacity of choice opportunities and implementation dynamics of priorities and preferences. As Thoenig and Paradieise [37] emphasize, "strategic capacity lies to a great extent in how much its internal subunits ... shape its identity, define its priorities approve its positions, prepare the way for general agreement to

DOI: http://dx.doi.org/10.5772/intechopen.81117

be adopted on its roadmap and provide a framework for the decisions and acts of all its components" (p. 299).

Such diverse views leave open how organizational identity, or shared central vision, confers competitive advantage in contested spaces. As a starting hypothesis, a shared identity strengthens coordination across diverse groups applying common norms, codes and protocols, hence improving shared learning skills. In a similar vein, individual cleavages and loyalties are lessoned by shared interactions and information sharing that mobilize learning tools. Further, organizational identity strengthens individual identities via performance success that promotes a shared set of preferences, expectation, and habits of rule setting.

3. Organizational performance at Toyota

By any standards—shareholder value, product innovation, employee satisfaction measured by low turnover and lack of strike action, market capitalization—Toyota has been astonishingly successful, both against rival incumbents in the auto sector, but as a organizational pioneer in transportation with just-in-time thinking. Against existing rivals at home, or in an industry with firms pursuing growth by alliances and acquisition (Renault-Nissan-Mitsubishi, VW-Porsche), facing receivership and saved by public funding (GM and Chrysler), exiting as a going concern (British Leyland) or new startups (Tesla). Toyota's performance is unrivaled. Toyota remains a firm committed to organic development, steady and consistent market share in all key international markets, and cultivating a shared identity within its eco-system around measurable outcomes of product safety, quality, and consumer value.

As shown in **Figure 1**, despite many forms of competitive advantages, such as size, high domestic market share, being part of a larger group, or diversification, there are many times when the side expected to win actually is less profitable and may actually lose. Toyota's growth and expansion, despite the turbulent 2009 recall and temporary retreats [38, 39], comes with consistent profitability and market share growth. In this organizational transformation, Toyota has replicated its

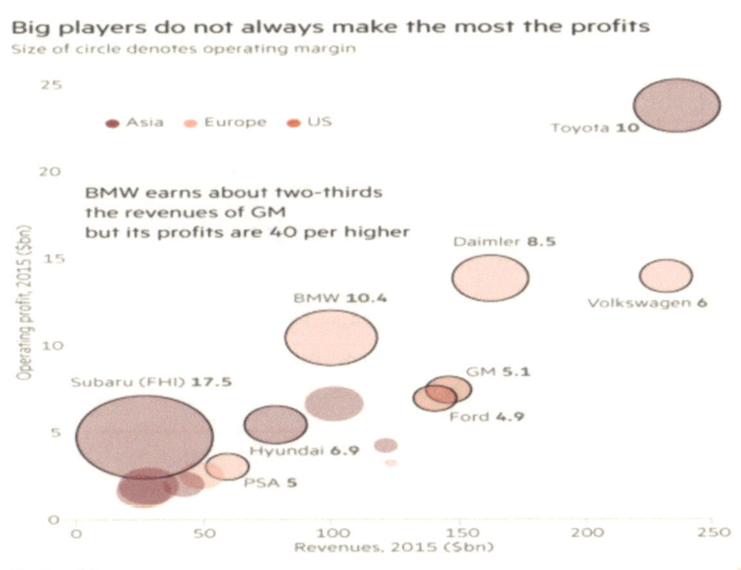

Figure 1.
Operating Profits versus Firm Revenues in the Auto Sector.

identity of "safety, quality, and value" outside its home market, often depicted by foreigners as "inscrutable," closed, and Japan Inc. [40]. Strategically, this organizational identity framework is multipurpose, allowing shared alignment of identities with domestic employees, suppliers and supervisors, but also incorporating these identity attributes first to foreign operations in North America and subsequently to Europe and Asia. Toyota management considers the firm as a learning organization, where learning symmetries take place at all levels, vertically and horizontally.

Unlike many corporate design models of multinationals, where foreign subsidiaries passively replicate the production systems of the home market (a miniature replica effect) or seek out decision-attention from head-quarters [41] Toyota is evolving as a global enterprise. In this model, Toyota's foreign subsidies and trade blocks (e.g., NAFTA and Europe), solve key problems and translate the protocols for headquarters and its global network of factories, distribution outlets, and service and maintenance dealerships. In this way, Toyota's training protocols, network learning systems, and using foreign subsidies to develop new technologies (e.g., Toyota Canada pioneering cold weather technologies for ignitions engineering), i.e., a learning chain that mobilizes employee identity to network identity, including its global supply chain collaboration [42–45].

To illustrate the complexity of contemporary auto production and the need to evolve both organizational design around supply chains, and the nature of complementarities in production, firms like Toyota must realign engineering and technological systems to novel role configurations for a diverse workforce. A car (or truck) has over 5000 parts, components, and sub-assemblies, where factories are linked to diverse supply chains with tightly-knit communications and transport linkages, often across national boundaries, to produce a factory production cycle of 1 minute per vehicle, or even less. Parts or components like steel, for instance, are not commodities, undifferentiated only by price, and Japanese steel producers produced the high carbon steel that was more resistant to water, hence rust. This production cycle demands very high quality and safety of each part and component, plus the precision engineering processes to assemble them. This alignment determines not only the standards of quality and safety of the finished vehicle but the image and reputation of the company, plus an indispensable need to retain price value of the brand in the aftermarket sales cycle.

To this contemporary production system, reshaped and refined since Toyota first introduced in 1956 what Womack et al. [46] termed "the machine that changed the world," auto production now faces a steady, relentless, and inexorable technology disruption. This shift in engines and fuel consumption technologies, away from diesel and gasoline-powered vehicles, to new dominant technologies, such as electric vehicles, fuel-cells, battery, hydrogen, or hybrid, each requiring massive changes to traditional parts and components suppliers, and the layout of factory assembly. Successful firms thus require forward-looking strategic intent and novel organizational configurations both to exploit existing systems based on gasoline vehicles, or novel organizational systems to explore new technologies and processes. Strategies differ widely. Tesla as a new startup has dedicated factories and labs using lithium battery technology. To gain equivalent scale of Toyota, GM, and Volkswagen, i.e., over 10 million vehicles per year, Nissan and Renault joined with Mitsubishi as a new alliances and equity investment partner.

By contrast, both Ford and GM are retreating from large markets like Europe, Japan, or India with direct-foreign investment strategies. Even more intrusive to existing production programs and protocols are new demands for data analytics, artificial intelligence, robotic and associated Internet and social media technologies. Both incumbent firms, new startups, and suppliers are developing futuristic technologies in drivers' facial recognition, driving habits, and consumer disabilities, from wheel chairs to hearing that impact cars of the future, and impose threats to existing distinctive competences and corporate identity. Not all firms can manage simultaneously the processes of exploitation of existing organizational programs, and the exploration of product innovation and assembly [47]. Toyota is an exception.

The Toyota production system is transformational, an organizational philosophy around two core ideas, *kaizen* or principles of continuous improvement, and *nemawashi*, or consensus decision-making that allow network effects across its global factories, research labs, its supplier organizations, and related parts of the global eco-system, from universities to global shipping firms. In the firm's century-old evolution, starting as a leading textile firm that still exists but migrating to auto manufacturing as only the second largest by unit sales (behind Nissan), Toyota has emerged as the top producer both at home and globally, measured by market share, and a leading player in markets like North America, Europe, Latin America, India and China, where many rivals have a low market share presence (e.g., Europe firms in the US, American firms in Europe).

Strategies of corporate retreat in key markets (GM in Europe, GM and Ford in India, Ford in Japan), suggest home market advantages are the new testing ground for first-mover disadvantage [48] when firms face massive technology disruption. To cite an example, during the 1990s, four major automakers, Toyota, GM, Honda, and Ford, took the lead in the development of hybrid technologies, with GM the leader with 23 patents in hybrid vehicles (vs. 17 for Toyota, 16 for Ford, and 8 for Honda). By 2000, however, Honda and Toyota were the clear leaders, with Honda had filed 170 patents, and Toyota with 166 in hybrid drivetrain technology, far ahead pf Ford with 85 and GM at 56. Today, Fords' hybrid is a license from Toyota.

4. Toyota identity as a social construct

The auto sector symbolizes the development of post-war multinationals largely based on firm-specific capabilities and proprietary advantages. This organizational evolution includes changing work mechanisms characterized as machine theory by management [49], a catch-all phrase to describe scientific management techniques espoused by Frederick Taylor from his 1911 book with that title. He first learned time management at Philips Executer Academy and became an early practitioner of what became known as *kaizen,* continuous improvement, working with Henry Gantt [50], studying all aspects of work, tools, machine speeds, workflow design, the conversion of raw materials into finished products, and payment systems. The Taylor studies, later dubbed *Fordism* [51], was an approach to eliminate waste and unnecessary movements, or "soldiering"—a deliberate restriction of worker output.

Taylor's disciples in the engineering profession spread his message beyond America, to Europe, as well as to Japan and Russia, where even Lenin and Trotsky developed an interest after the Revolution of 1917. In appearances before Congressional committees, and in other forums, Taylor's theories faced withering criticisms and great resistance by American union movement a "dehumanizing of the worker" and a tool for profits at the expense of the worker. [50, 52]. In Japan, however, Taylorism and scientific management had wide acceptance, starting with Yukinori Hoshino's translation of *Principles of Scientific Management* with the title, *The Secret of Saving Lost Motion,* which sold 2 million copies. Several firms adopted scientific management practices, including standard motions, worker bonuses, and Japanese authors published best sellers on similar notions of work practices, including one entitled *Secrets for Eliminating Futile Work and Increasing Production* [3].

After 1945 in Japan, given the wartime devastation of Japan's industrial capacity, resource scarcity—food, building supplies, raw materials of all sorts, electric power—had a profound and lasting impact on Japanese society, even more so when the American military supervised the Occupation and displayed abundance of everyday goods—big cars, no shortage of food, long leisure hours, and consumer spending using American dollars. As Japanese firms slowly rebuilt, the corporate ethos promoted efficient use of everything, and waste became a watchword for inefficiency. Japanese executives visited US factories, the Japanese media documented US success stories. American management practices were widely emulated, and US consultants—notably Peter Drucker, W. Juran, and W. Edwards Deming—had an immense following and their books, papers and personal appearances were publicized, translated and widely-read, even by high school students. While American firms emphasized a marketing philosophy where the customer is king, Japanese firms remained committed to production, helped in part by trading firms, led by the nine giant *Soga Sosha*, to distribute and sell both at home and abroad. US human resource practices also showed a stark contrast with Japanese practices. In the US, the rise of the trade union movement and national legislation from Roosevelt's New Deal, meant that management-worker relations for firms and factories were contractual, setting out legal norms, and negotiated commitments for pay, seniority, promotion, job rotation and skills differentials, so that worker identity was less towards the firm, more to the trade union, and what incentives and compensation union leadership could deliver [53].

Japan industrial firms, by contrast, cultivated three features of management-worker relations. The first was life time employment—once hired, the employee stayed in the firm until retirement. Second, wages and compensation were determined by seniority—young workers received lower wages and bonus compensation, just as older workers were paid more relative to their actual productivity. And third, firms had enterprise unions, as distinct from industry unions in the US and Europe (e.g., unions autoworkers, coal workers or shipbuilders). All three characteristics greatly extended the psychological linkages between employee identity and the firm's identity, and the employee's career success was directly tied to the firm's success. In Japan, with very low turnover, but high screening processes, firms hired the best graduates, and training was on-going and formed part of the job description, with little layoffs, firing, or absenteeism. Additionally, there was little employee fear of adopting new technologies. Abegglen and Stalk [54] describe the implication of technological diffusion as follows: "...it is the relatively close identification of the interests of *kaisha* and their employees that have made this rate of technological change possible and the patterns of union relations implicit in that degree of identification" (p. 133). Indeed, some writers go further, citing how the human resource system was imposed on a Confucian society, with an ethos to govern individual and group interactions for reciprocal benefits, in a market system of winners and losers. As Morishima [55] puts it, Korea and China chose Confucianism with the market, Japan chose the market with Confucianism, while North America and Europe were characterized by Protestant-driven market behavior of winners and losers. For Toyota, a family enterprise with links to many sectors like steel, textiles, aviation and machinery, the post-war environment brought inevitable contracts with American automotive practices.

Okika [56] describes the implications of the evolving Japanese model of labor-management relations in the firm:

> *Japanese enterprises made their decisions by gaining an overall consensus through repeated discussions starting from the bottom and working up ... making it easier for workers to accept technical innovation flexibly. For a start, that sense of identity with the firm is strong and they are aware that the firm's development is to their own advantage, so they tend to improve the efficiency of its production system and strengthens its competitiveness (p. 22).*

DOI: http://dx.doi.org/10.5772/intechopen.81117

Across Japan, industrial firms, from Sony to Canon, recruited workers from rural areas, executives read US textbooks, and many visited US factories to study management practices. The production focus of Japanese firms, in a competitive environment of limited slack, hence the need for managerial improvisation and what the French call *bricolage*, i.e., making do with what is available [57]. In operational terms, this meant long production runs, division of labor taken to the extreme is monotonous assembly work tasks, product output determined by managerial estimates of demand, and wide use of buffer stocks to absorb varying time cycles of different sub-assembly needs. Buffer stocks also allowed conflicting management department goals to get sorted out with little time constraints, and less need to focus on quality issues based on bad product design, resource waste (e.g., steel), or timing processes that lead to product defects. Organizational reforms widely adopted across US industry, such as product divisions for large enterprises, largely left the product system intact, allowing middle management to focus on coordination between operational benchmarks at the factory level and financial benchmarks imposed by top management [58]. GM was seen in Japan as the prototype models to emulate.

5. Challenges to orthodox industrial production

The advance of industrialization involved new methods of energy, raw materials, dominant technologies, and organizational configurations [58] but relatively little to consideration actual production systems, especially after Henry Ford introduced mass production using interchangeable parts. As foreign executives visited Ford's assembly lines, there were dissenting opinions, such as Czech entrepreneur Thomas Bata and S. Toyoda who worked a year in Detroit. How could three core concepts be integrated—craft skills of custom-made products like a *kimono* or a house, the volume-cost advantages of mass production, and the nigh utilization capacity of process production in beer or chemicals?

Toyota's introduction of the lean production system has been widely studied,[2] including its the origins in the 1950s by Ohno [62], when visiting America and adopting ideas from super market chains, and had strong views on scientific management's focus on the total production system, and Japanese concepts of *jishu kanri* (voluntary work groups). Japanese managers had both knowledge and experience with traditional crafts sectors like woodblock prints and silk designs in textiles or the long training needed for Japan's culinary arts. How could three core concepts be integrated—craft skills of custom-made products like a *kimono* or a house, the volume-cost advantages of mass production, and the nigh utilization capacity of process production in beer or chemicals?

Core concepts of lean production is the desire to maximize capacity utilization, by reducing production variability and minimize excess inventories with a view to eradicating waste [54]. But other factors are critical, such as supplying high quality workmanship of craft production, reducing per unit costs via mass production using interchangeable parts, and high capacity utilization of continuous flow production, typically seen as three distinct systems. The ingrained ethos of resource scarcity in Japanese society, demonstrating that low slack in organizations encourage search behavior [63], and these requirements required pooling of efforts as an organizational philosophy (**Figure 2**).

---

[2] For more detailed background on Toyota's production system, see Cusumano [59], Dyer and Nobeoka [43], Fujimoto [60], Likert [61], McMillan [3], and Ohno [62].

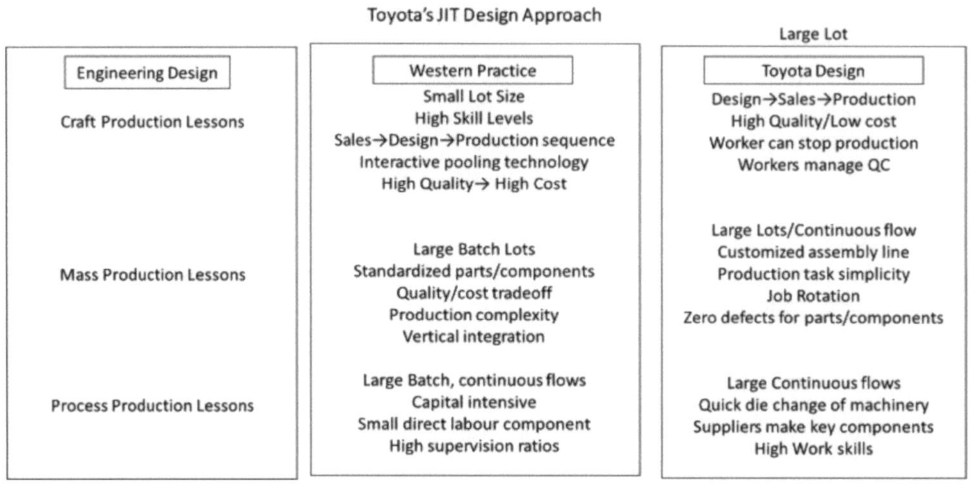

Figure 2.
Contrasts Between Traditional Technical Design and Toyota's Model.

To perfect the system over time, starting in the 1960s, Toyota accelerated the adoption of high work commitment by organizing workers in teams, reducing the number of job classifications, seeking suggestions from employees, and investing in training of new workers, 47–48 days per worker, compared to less than 5–6 days for US plants, 21–22 days for European plants [3]. The focus on production as an integrated system, using hardware ideas like quick die change equipment, robots, and advanced computer-aided design, also meant removing traditional tasks that are noisy, hard on the eyes, or dangerous to allow employees to concentrate on tasks like quality assessment, and allowing a worker to stop the entire production line, known as *andon,* in the case of equipment problems, shortage of parts, and discovery of defects, i.e., transferring certain responsibilities from managers and supervisors to workers [60]. Paradoxically, Toyota and other Japanese auto plants were far less automated than their foreign-owned rivals, not just for assembly line work but other tasks like welding and painting.

Einstein once said, "Make everything as simple as possible, but no simpler." Simplicity became a watchword in the evolution of Toyota's lean production system, a contrast to the complicated vertical integration model adopted in Detroit. Toyota adopted a highly focused structural design, becoming a systems assembler and sourcing from dedicated suppliers, each with core competences in specialized domains and technologies. Production engineering—e.g., craft, mass assembly or process systems—became central features as organizational configuration, choosing from the strengths of each but discarding the perceived weaknesses. Stress was place on the worker, avoiding the monotonous routines of a moving assembly line, by including job rotation and special training to apply quality management circles within a group structure. The advantages of process manufacturing as high capacity utilization came from high initial overhead of equipment and overhead, including IT investments, but allowing flexibility in machine set up, such as quick die change that reduced the need to stop the line for product variability from 3 months, to 3 weeks, to 3 minutes, to less than 3 seconds. The internal factory layout, an S shape configuration, changed the sequencing of tasks, the forms of supervisor-employee interactions, and the speed and timing of interdependencies between the production operations and external suppliers of parts, delivering "just in time."

In some cases, the interactions involve the core production system and independent suppliers serving as complementarities[3] where the competitive advantage of one is augmented by the presence of the other [45]. Early examples included Ford's cooperation with Firestone to produce tires, or Renault's links to Michelin to produce radial tires. Complementarities allow synergistic advantages, a contrast to additive, discrete features [64], and allow two immediate effects: knowledge spillovers at differing stages of production, including process learning impacts, and complimentary and coordinated changes in activities and programs across the value chain, such as process benchmarks for product design, scheduling, inspection, and time cycles of production. Toyota cultivates complementarity attributes but instituted a revised activity sequence, discarding production based on estimated demand forecasts, and turning finished production of cars and trucks to car lots for ultimate sale. The pull system starts with customer demands, allowing novel design using the advantages of the need for high capacity utilization of smaller actual output demands, to manufacture outputs with shorter time for product delivery.

6. JIT and Toyota's deep supplier collaboration systems

Toyota's lean production both reconfigures the boundaries of the firm by incorporating the supply chain as an integrated, cooperative network with collective competences and capabilities across the network value chain and incorporates decision processes for learning and knowledge sharing that shifts subunit identities to a collective identity. Lean production requires these system-wide processes to address inoperability issues like buffer stocks, time delays, peak demand, or product defects. Deep collaboration across sub-units needs robust methods to design, evaluate, and verify data gathering and data feedback. Unlike economic models of transaction costs, or contractual relations, lean production emphasizes symmetrical collaboration to optimize outcome effectiveness for the total eco-system organization, not sub-optimize for only certain members, sub-units, or component firms. Toyota's collective identity is a notable corporate example that combines both superb operational performance but also long-term, forward looking innovation through its complex ecosystem of Tier I and Tier II supplier system. As depicted in **Figure 3**, Toyota aligns its supply system both domestically and overseas with knowledge systems, including standards of precision and quality, including using internal staffing and consultants to assure optimum outcomes against agreed benchmarks.

By replacing asymmetric contractual relations based on cost, Toyota shifts the locus of corporate risk to the total eco-system, involving Toyota at the center, the Tier I and Tier II suppliers, and their Tier I and Tier II suppliers. The lean "pull" of production control is a connectivity to calibrate inventory at each stage, starting with the final assembly and preceding to each preceding stage without delay. Unlike the push model, where the early steps of sub-assembly is sequential to subsequent stages and require buffer inventory to lesson delays, Toyota's lean system of 'pulling' requires training and upgrading skills employed at different work stations, and close

[3] In mass assembly industries like autos, shipbuilding, and heavy construction equipment, where steel is a complementary component, scale, technology, and technical systems, including plant location, largely define cost advantages. By the early 1980s, the competitive gap between Japan and the US was increasing, just as Japanese firms were shifting from export strategies to direct foreign investment, i.e. establishing new plants in North America with the newest equipment, sourcing, and lean production. One analysis showed the contrast: "... the American steel industry had fallen from the largest and most technologically advanced in the world to the condition of a lagging competitor ... companies retrofitted new technology unto often antiquated facilities" ([49], p. 91).

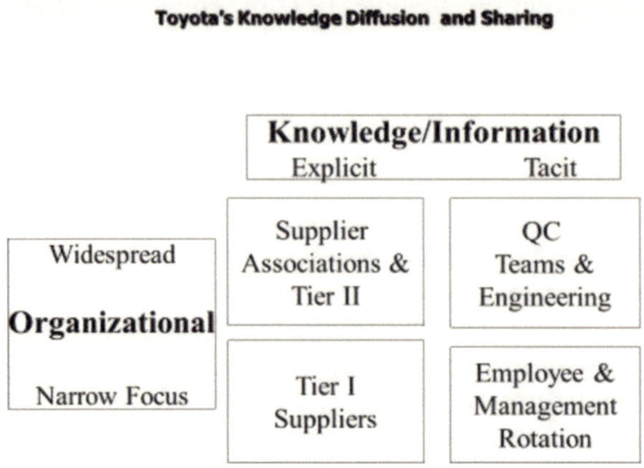

Figure 3.
Toyota's Knowledge Diffusion and Sharing Approaches.

communications across the total supply chain system. To make this system work, economic transaction costs are discarded, and replaced by a currency of cooperation using preventive tools and benchmarks to meet high standards of reliability where Tier II firms meet rigorous standards of price, quality, and delivery. Suppliers are battle-tested, i.e., they must conform to agreed specifications and their products are accepted only after years of testing. Tier I suppliers, on the other hand, meet the exacting standards of Tier II suppliers but they form part of the design, research, and testing of new products, markets, and technological innovations. Tier II suppliers can "graduate" to being Tier I suppliers if they meet benchmark performance over time, thus demanding intense deep collaboration at Level 4 (**Figure 4**).

Less coordinated systems of structure, processes, and executive decision-making inhibit eco-system operability. Three integrating systems are vital: (1) technical systems, including IT, software, and data; (2) organizational tools of coordination, like dedication teams supported by specialists and intense data sharing; and (3) collaborative executive decision processes that champion novelty, innovation, and feedback [65, 66]. Inoperability can come from seemingly mundane tasks, like loading supplies on a truck with different invoices, manifest requirements, and

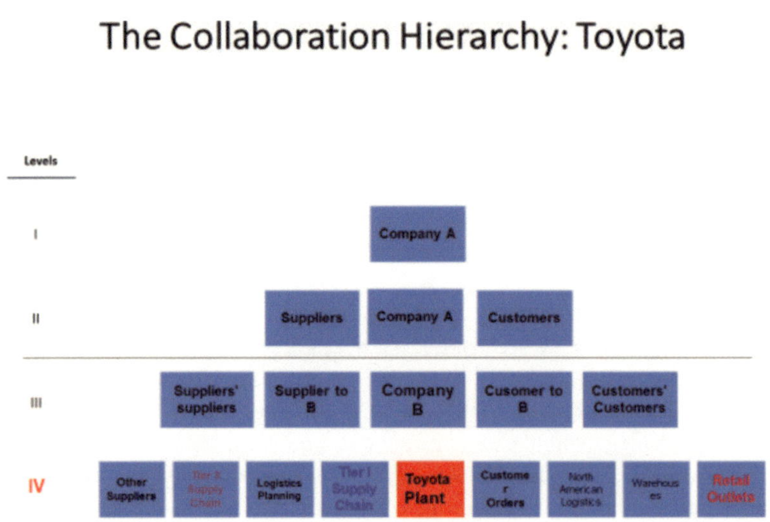

Figure 4.
Levels of Value Chain Collaboration: Toyota as Level 4.

delivery times. Separate and differing organizational processes inhibit deep collaboration. Inoperability arises from silo information flows and compartmentalization. Even with aspirational targets of decision-making, organizations acting alone fail to develop and improve competencies and capabilities to manage this integrated system via experiential learning, feedback, and criticism [67–69].

Deep collaboration needs robust methods to design, evaluate, and verify data gathering and data feedback to optimize effectiveness for the total eco-system organization, not sub-optimize for only certain members, sub-parts, or component firms [70]. Toyota's lean production now has both a language and a vocabulary to remove task ambiguities and increase identity among workers, sub-units, and factories in the global network, but requiring a learning process to perfect clear meanings and defined protocols. Words like *kanban, andon, jioda, yo-i-dan,* and *kijosei* have precise meanings and routines, and such terms as reverse engineering, early detection, and *ringi seido* or consensus decision-making, simplify and codify precise protocols for shared communication. Benchmark techniques are widely used but less to evaluate past performance against competitors, but more to evaluate current performance against higher targets and aspirational stretch goals [71]. Indeed, deep collaboration at each stage requires a judicious combination of sharing ideas, new targets, real time feedback, and potential revisions. Where ambiguous signals, informal targets and past measures become explicit, and shared across the system.

Training programs—internships, formal courses, apprenticeships—build organizational capabilities and mitigates risks from operating with incomplete knowledge, inexperience, understanding operating rules and procedures. Deep collaboration illustrates the need for similar training approaches to know, understand, and apply knowledge across the entire system. Toyota gains three network advantages: positional, where individual managers and subsidiaries access tools and protocols for high performance processes and benchmarks that create learning; structural, where communication connections strengthen the effectiveness and acuity of information flows to attend to emerging problems; agility, by strengthening interactions between individuals and teams, and embedding the new benchmarks across the entire network of factories, sales offices, and supplier organizations.

7. Split identities at Toyota

By the early 1980s, Toyota, like many leading Japanese corporations such as Sony, Komatsu, Canon, Matsushita, and Hitachi, were making deep inroads in the American market via exports. The auto sector was singled out, as 500,000 American autoworkers were laid off, a new President, Ronald Reagan faced pressure from Congress to take legislative action, and firms like Ford applied to the American International Trade Commission for temporary relief, following similar action by the powerful auto union, the UAW. Further, Japan's emphasis on direct export sales stood in contrast to American strategies of direct investment in foreign markets, often by acquisition of local companies [8, 45, 72] .[4] For firms like Toyota,

[4] In one of the great ironies of business history, in the 1930s, when Ford and General Motors provided two-thirds of the Japanese car market, mostly by assembling kits from their home market, the Japanese government, despite their desire to focus on auto production, wanted Ford to establish a joint-venture with Toyota. Various agreements were planned, including land purchase, but Ford, denied permission to expand local production on its own, retreated from Japan in 1939, followed by GM [73]. In 1980, China invited Toyota to establish a joint venture, but when Toyota decided not to accept, China turned to Volkswagen, not by far the most successful foreign carmaker, producing 4 million units, in a market of 2 million a month. Toyota produces only 1 million per year.

growing high dependence on exports meant that larger total volumes (domestic + exports) strengthened their product capacity and cost position at home, including that of their supplier base. Japan's auto exports to the US reached 6.6 million vehicles in 1981, up from a million units 10 years earlier, 566,042, accounted for almost 20% of total Japanese auto exports.

The imposition of Japan's export restraints, formalized in June 1981, coincided a $1.5b loan guarantee to Chrysler, indefinite layoffs of over 30,000 auto workers, and sectors like steel facing declining market share. Pressed by firms like Ford for Congressional actions, MITI imposed export quotas on each Japanese company, a form of "administrative guidance" designed to accommodate political goals in each country but was in fact a "cartel" solution aimed to appease the US government [3, 74]. The percentage breakdown for each of the five biggest exporters, calculated mainly by US exports in the previous 2 years, was as follows: Toyota (30.75), Nissan (27.15), Honda (20.75), Mazda (9.48), and Mitsubishi (6.7). The impact for each company in the brutally competitive Japanese market varied: Honda was the first to begin direct investment, opening its first plant in Ohio and then Ontario; while Toyota kept to its quota by exports but strengthened domestic operations to build up a commanding market share lead, over 50%. For the Japanese auto sector, as Summerville notes [74], "investment in local production was also a crucial way to insulate oneself from further export cutbacks, and of course to get away from the thumb of the Japanese state" (p. 395). Toyota illustrates the complexity to manage very fast growth in foreign markets, while transferring its corporate identity to a network identity of safety, quality, and value [43], even though the knowledge sharing processes that are now taken for granted at home, including quality standards of suppliers, may not exist in foreign countries [75–78].

The massive recall in 1999, where Toyota accepted responsibility to service over 8.5 million vehicles, the President appearing before Congress, and sundry lawsuits launched in a litigious environment against a foreign-owned firm, have been analyzed and studied[5] in the media, the automotive press, and by academic studies, with mixed conclusions. The reality, despite paying fines, accepting responsibility, apologizing to the American public, and accepting the huge financial costs of the recall, Toyota refused to play the blame game, or take easy solutions, like importing more parts from Canada or Japan, or shifting American production to Canada or Mexico. Toyota took the difficult decision, true to its identity, of fixing the core problem, raising the quality standards of its American-own parts supplier, devoting more resources to training, and accepting short-term risks to financial performance, particularly when leading automakers from Europe, Korea, and Japan were investing in the US market. The Detroit Big 3 received temporary relief, a massive bailout after bankruptcy from the US and Canadian government, and a 25% tariff on imported trucks, one of the most profitable segments for American producers. Toyota quietly responded about building a truck factory in Texas.

8. Discussion and conclusions

In a world of disruptive corporate strategy and identity offer a refined tool for alignment of stakeholders to create competitive advantage. Corporate culture focuses on the behavioral assumptions to perceive, think, and feel in

[5] For background, see Andrews et al. [79], Camuffo and Wilhelm [39], and Cole [80].

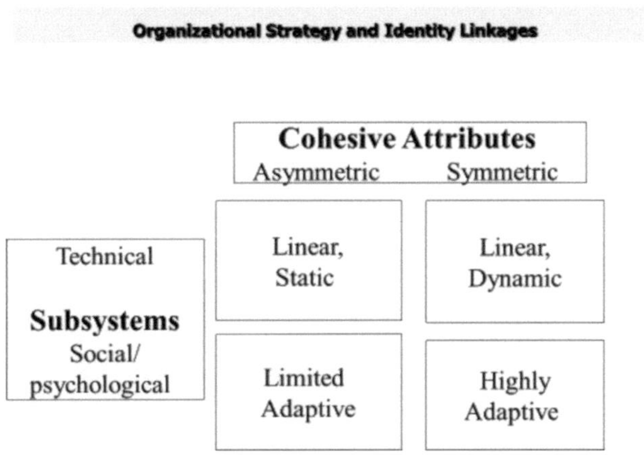

Figure 5.
Organizational Strategy and Identity Linkages.

problem-solving [81] within the organization, while organizational identity is a projection of that culture to external stakeholders to align both cognitive and behavioral tools for growth and innovation. Individual and sub-unit identities can lead to cleavage and discord, especially where environmental forces make knowledge and information asymmetric, so special attention and sense-making requires an adaptive alignment to improve performance (**Figure 5**).

Increasing, all organizations face four separate but related challenges that impact overall performance but also survival as independent entities. Clearly, technological change imposes new challenges for internal organizational competences and capabilities, as firms scramble for mergers, takeovers, and new alliances to meet the test of size and foreign market penetration, or a retreat approach or even drift. Decision uncertainty influences the nature of internal competencies, learning barriers, and the sustainable position of existing firms. The third challenge with disruption is the growing complexity of the firm's ecosystem, and what is the optimal scale of a firm's future business case, based on potential changes to customer markets across multiple countries?

The fourth challenge relates to the first three but is subtler. That challenge concerns what might be called the Galapagos trap, namely designing an ecosystem that is suitable for one market that is unsuitable for global markets and allows little transfer of knowledge or engineering knowhow to other markets with a separate eco-system, including the supplier system. Recent examples include Japan's unique wireless standards that did not apply in foreign markets systems, or American big car gas guzzlers with limited fuel mileage that did not meet foreign market regulations. Toyota's development of hydrogen fuel powered vehicles, based on new chemical technologies, is a case in point, where existing infrastructure lacks the necessary technical requirements for even limited mass appeal. In all four of these development challenges, the competitive race is to avoid the lessons of the computer industry, where new smart phone technologies displaced existing incumbents, lowered entry barriers for new startups, and shifted the main suppliers and their location.

Such fundamental changes pose difficult questions for firms' missions, corporate identity, and framing long term employee loyalty. As Simon [76] warned decades ago, "organizational identification...implies absorption of strategic plans into the minds of organizational members where they can have direct effect upon the entire decision-process, starting with the identification of problems..." (p. 141).

Author details

Charles McMillan
Schulich School of Business, York University, Toronto, Canada

*Address all correspondence to: charlesmcmillansgi@gmail.com

References

[1] Toyota Motor Corporation. The Toyota Production System. Tokyo: Japan; 1992

[2] Takeuchi H, Osono E, Shimizu N. The contradictions that affect Toyota's success. Harvard Business Review. 2008;(June):96-104

[3] McMillan CJ. The Japanese Industrial System. Berlin: De Gruyter; 1985

[4] Spear S, Bowen HH. Decoding the DNA of the Toyota production system. Harvard Business Review. 1999;**87**:97-106

[5] Stuart A, Whetten DA. Organizational identity. Research in Organizational Behavior. 1985;**7**:263-295

[6] Hatch MJ, Schultz M. Organizational Identity: A Reader. Oxford: Oxford University Press; 2004

[7] He H, Brown AD. Organizational identity and organizational identification: A review of the literature and suggestions for research. Group and Organization Management. 2013;**38**(1):3-35

[8] McMillan C, Overall J. Crossing the chasm and over the abyss: Perspectives on organizational failure. Academy of Management Perspectives. 2017;**31**(4):1-17

[9] Whetton DA. Albert and Whetton revisited, strengthening the concept of organizational identity. Journal of Management Inquiry. 2006;**15**:119-134

[10] Rodrigues S, Child J. The development of corporate identity: A political perspective. Journal of Management Studies. 2008;**45**:885-911

[11] Schultz M, Maguire S, Langley A, Tsoukas H. Constructing Identity in and around Organizations. Oxford, UK: Oxford University Press; 2012

[12] Balmer JMT, Greyser SA. Managing the multiple identities of the Corporation. California Management Review. 2002;**44**(3):72-86

[13] Kogut B. Knowledge, Options, and Institutions. Oxford: Oxford University Press; 2008. https://www.amazon.com/s/ref=rdr_ext_aut?_encoding=UTF8&index=books&field-author=Bruce Kogut

[14] Durkheim E. The Division of Labour in Society. New York: Free Press; 1933

[15] Camuffo A, Wilhelm M. Complementarities and organizational (Mis)fit: A retrospective analysis of the Toyota recall crisis. Journal of Organizational Design. 2016;**5**:2-13

[16] Simon HA. Administrative Behavior. New York: MacMillan; 1976

[17] March JG, Simon HA. Organizations. New York: John Wiley; 1958

[18] Katz D, Kahn RL. The Social Psychology of Organizations. New York: Wiley; 1966

[19] Hofstede G. Culture's Consequences. Beverley Hills, CA: Sage Publishing; 1980

[20] Giddens A. Modernity and Self-identity: Self and Society in the Late Modern Age. Stanford, CA: Stanford University Press; 1988

[21] Vough H, Caza BB. Identity work in organizations and occupations: Definitions, theories, and pathways forward. Journal of Organizational Behavior. 2018;**39**(7):889-910. https://scholar.google.ca/scholar?oi=bibs&cluster=17457274272124570525&btnI=1&hl=en

[22] Hammack PL. Narrative and the cultural psychology of identity.

Personnel and Social Psychology Review. 2008;**12**(3):222-247

[23] Dutton JE, Dukerich JM, Harquail CV. Organizational images and member identification. Administrative Science Quarterly. 1994;**39**:239-263

[24] Alvesson M, Ashcraft KL, Thomas R. Identity matters: Reflections on the construction of identity scholarship in organization studies. Organization. 2008;**15**:5-28

[25] Lamertz K, Pursey PM, Heugens AR, Calmet L. The configuration of organizational images among firms in the Canadian Beer Brewing Industry. Journal of Management Studies. 2005;**42**(4):817-843. https://onlinelibrary.wiley.com/action/doSearch?ContribAuthorStored=Lamertz%2C+Kai, https://onlinelibrary.wiley.com/action/doSearch?ContribAuthorStored=Heugens%2C+Pursey+P+M+A+R, https://onlinelibrary.wiley.com/action/doSearch?ContribAuthorStored=Calmet%2C+Loïc

[26] Hirschman AO. Exit, Voice and Loyalty: Responses to Decline in Firms Organizations, and States. Cambridge: Harvard University Press; 1970

[27] Akerlof GA, Kranton RE. Identity and the economics of organizations. Journal of Economic Perspectives. 2005;**19**:9-32

[28] Likert R. New Patterns of Management. New York: McGraw-Hill; 1961. p. 1961

[29] Dutton JE, Dukerich JM. Keeping an eye on the mirror: The role of image andidentity in organizational adaptation. Academy of Management Journal.1991;**34**:517-554

[30] Elsbach KD, Kramer RM. Members' responses to organizational identity threats: Encountering and countering the Business Week rankings. Administrative Science Quarterly. 1996;**41**:442-476

[31] Martin J, Frost PJ, O'neill OA. Organizational culture: Beyond struggles for intellectual dominance. In: The SAGE Handbook of Organization Studies. Newbury Park, CA: SAGE Publications; 2016. https://www.gsb.stanford.edu/faculty-research/faculty/joanne-martin

[32] Prentice DA, Carranza E. What women and men should be, shouldn't be, are allowed to be, and don't have to be: The contents of prescriptive gender stereotypes. Psychology of Women Quarterly. 2002;**26**(4):269-281

[33] House R, Iavidan M, Hanges P, Dorfman PW. Understanding cultures and implicit leadership theories across the Globe: An introduction to project GLOBE. Journal of World Business. 2002;**37**(1):3-10

[34] Goldthorpe JH. The Affluent Worker: Industrial Attitudes and Behaviour. Cambridge: Cambridge University Press; 1968

[35] O'Reilly C, Chatman JA. Culture as social control: Corporations, cults, and commitment. In: Staw BM, Cummings LL, editors. Research in Organizational Behavior. Vol. 18, Greenwich, CT: JAI Press, Inc.; 1996

[36] Cremer J. Corporate culture and shared knowledge. Industrial and Corporate Change. 1993;**2**(3):351-386s

[37] He H, Brown AD. Organizational identity and organizational identification: A review of the literature and suggestions for research. Group and Organization Managemen*t*. 2013;**38**(1):3-35

[38] Cole R. What really happened to Toyota? MIT Sloan Management Review. 2011;**52**(4):29-35

[39] Camuffo A, Wilhelm M. Complementarities and organizational (Mis)fit: A retrospective analysis of the Toyota recall crisis. Journal of Organizational Design. 2016;**5**:2-13

[40] van Wolferen K. The Enigma of Japanese Power: People and Politics in a Stateless Nation. New York: Vintage Books; 1990

[41] Bouquet C, Birkinshaw J. Managing power in the multinational Corporation. Journal of Management. 2008;**34**:477-508

[42] Adler PS, Goldoftas B, Levine D. Flexibility versus efficiency? A case study of model changeovers in the Toyota, production system. Organizational Science. 1999;**10**(1):43-68

[43] Dyer JH, Nobeoka K. Creating and managing a high performance knowledge-sharing network: The Toyota case. Strategic Management Journal. 2000;**21**:345-367

[44] Fruin WM, Nishiguchi T. Supplying the Toyota production system: Intercorporate organizational evolution and supplier subsystems. In: Kogut B, editor. Country Competitiveness. Oxford: Oxford University Press; 1993. pp. 225-246

[45] Paul M, Roberts J. The economics of modern manufacturing: Technology, strategy, and organization. American Economic Review. 1990;**89**(3):511-528

[46] Liker J. The Toyota Way: 14 Management Principles from the world's Greatest Manufacturer. New York: McGraw-Hill; 2004

[47] March JG. Explorations in Organizations. Stanford: Stanford University Press; 2008

[48] Saurez F, Lanzolla G. The role of environmental dynamics in building a first move advantage theory. Academy of Management Review. 2007;**32**(2):377-392

[49] McGraw TK, O'Brien PA. Production and distribution: competition and industry structure. In: McGraw TK, editor. America versus Japan. Boston: Harvard Business School Press; 1986

[50] Aitken HGJ. Taylorism at Waterton Arsenal: Scientific Management in Action 1908-1915. Cambridge: Harvard University Press; 1960

[51] Amin A, editor. Post-Fordism—A Reader. Oxford: Blackwell Publishers; 2000

[52] McMillan C. Five forces for effective leadership and innovation. Journal of Business Strategy. 2010;**31**:11-22

[53] Bendix R. Work and Authority in Industry: Ideologies of Management in the Course of Industrialization. New York: Routledge; 1956

[54] Abegglen J, Stalk G. Kaisha: The Japanese Corporation. Basic Books; 1985. http://www.amazon.com/Kaisha-Japanese-Corporation-James-Abegglen/dp/0465037119

[55] Morishima M. Why Has Japan 'Succeeded'? Cambridge: Cambridge University Press; 1982

[56] Okika S. Japan in the World Economy. Tokyo: University of Tokyo Press; 1989

[57] Lévi-Strauss C. The Savage Mind. Chicago: University of Chicago Press; 1962

[58] Morishima M. Why Has Japan 'Succeeded'? Cambridge: Cambridge University Press; 1982

[59] Nonaka I, Toyama R, Hirata T. Managing Flow: A Process Theory of the Knowledge-Based Firm. New York: Palgrave MacMillan; 2008

[60] Fujimoto T. The Evolution of a Manufacturing System at Toyota. New York: Oxford University Press; 1999

[61] Liker J. The Toyota Way: 14 Management Principles from the world's Greatest Manufacturer. New York: McGraw-Hill; 2004

[62] Ohno T. Toyota Production System: Beyond Large-Scale Production. Cambridge: Productivity Press; 1988

[63] Cyert R, March JG. A Behavioral Theory of the Firm. Englewood Cliffs: Prentice-Hall; 1963

[64] Enman E, Richter A. The whole is more than the sum of its parts—Or is it? A review of the empirical literature on complementarities in organizations. Journal of Management. 2010;**36**(1):207-233

[65] Asanuma B. Manufacturer-supplier relationships in Japan and the concept of relation-specific skill. Journal of the Japanese and International Economies. 1989;**3**(1):1-30

[66] Nonaka I, Toyama R, Hirata T. Managing Flow: A Process Theory of the Knowledge-Based Firm. New York: Palgrave MacMillan; 2008

[67] Kogut B, Zander U. What firms do? Coordination, identity and learning. Organization Science. 1996;**7**:502-518

[68] Liker J, Hoseus M. Toyota Culture. The Heart and Soul of the Toyota Way. New York: McGraw Hill; 2008

[69] McMillan C. Five forces for effective leadership and innovation. Journal of Business Strategy. 2010;**31**:11-22

[70] Sako S. Supplier development at Honda, Nissan and Toyota: Comparative case studies of organizational capability enhancement. Industrial & Corporate Change. 2004;**13**(2):281-308

[71] Iyer AV, Seshshodrig S, Roy V. Toyota Supply Chain Management. New York: McGraw-Hill; 2009

[72] McMillan C. Old wine in new bottles: Docility, attention scarcity, and knowledge management. Journal of Knowledge Management. 2016;**20**:1-21

[73] Sundelson JW. U.S. automotive investments abroad. In: Kindleberger C editor. The International Corporation. Cambridge: MIT Press; 1970

[74] Simon HA. Strategy and organizational evolution. Strategic Management Journal. 1993;**14**(2):131-142

[75] McMillan C. An integrated framework to orchestrate long term competitive advantage. International Journal of Strategic Management. 2017;**17**:75-92. DOI: 10.18374/IJSM-17-2.6

[76] Stalk GJ, Hout TM. Competing Against Time: How Time-Based Competition is Reshaping Global Markets. New York: Free Press; 1990

[77] Vernon R. International investment and international trade in the product cycle. Quarterly Journal of Economics. 1966;**80**:190-207

[78] Taira K. Labour market segmentation, human resources utilization, and economic development: The case of Japan in historical perspective. In: Sato R, Negishi T, editors. Developments in Japanese Economics. Tokyo: Academic Press; 1989

[79] Andrews AP, Simon J, Tian F, Zhao J. The Toyota crisis: An economic, operational and strategic analysis of the massive recall. Management Research Review. 2011;**34**(10):1064-1077

[80] Toyota Motor Corporation. The Toyota Production System. Tokyo: Japan; 1992

[81] Schein EH. Organizational Culture and Leadership. San Francisco: Jossey-Bass; 1998

Chapter 6

Risk Management Techniques

Hafeth I. Naji, Rouwaida Hussein Ali
and Ehsan Ali Al-Zubaidi

Abstract

The importance of risk management has been increasing for a lot of construction projects in different industries, and thus risk management department must be established to monitor the risks. The construction industry and its managers are exposed to a high degree of risk that leads to increasing the cost or delay in the projects. Therefore, there must be techniques used to control the risk and determine the best method to respond to it. Artificial intelligence and its techniques will be described includes the principle of and its advantages, types and the techniques that used for the classification that includes, decision tree and K-star, neural network and support vector machine and simulation techniques like system dynamic and also using optimization techniques, Particle swarm, Gravitational Search Algorithm as follows: Classification (decision tree, K-star, neural network, support vector. Machine and).

Keywords: risk, risk management, techniques, classification, neural network

1. Introduction

The concept of risk management includes two parts: the first one is the management, and the meaning of management is planning, organizing, and protecting; while the other part which is risk is the variability of what is expected [1].

Risk management is defined as the process that is able to find the risks and analyze these risks using a suitable method and then put the appropriate response to eliminate those risks or reduce them, thereby increasing the success of the project and the achievement of its goals [2].

Risk management is also defined as the process that enables the analysis and management of risks related to the project and its aim is to reduce the risk that threatens the goal of the project and hence it takes the responsibility of increasing the opportunity for the competition of the project in time, cost, and quality [3]. Risk management techniques are considered to be very important and there are a lot of techniques, especially artificial intelligent techniques.

Artificial intelligence is defined as the process of studying systems which behave in an intelligent manner as an observer to another. AI includes the use of tools depending on the intelligent behavior of human beings and other animals too in order for the complex problems [4].

AI is interested in artifacts intelligent behavior, which includes understanding, thinking, learning, communicating, and working in environments which are complex. In general, the utmost objective of AI is the process of perceiving the development of tools and mechanisms that can behave as humans behave or even better. Another objective of AI can be known which can as comprehension behavior, whether it appears in machines or in humans that mean simulate the human's behaviors. Thus, AI contains both scientific and engineering objectives [5]. Various references discover in the scientific literature that artificial intelligence integrates with project management areas are based on the artificial intelligence, project success estimation, critical success factors identification, project budget Relatedness, project schedule connection planning of the project, and risk identification relatedness [6].

Artificial intelligence include the classification techniques.

2. Classification

Classification, as described in statistics and machine learning, is the identification of a group of categories (subpopulations) to identify a new category, depending on the o training set of data that have the same instance whose classes are already known. For instance, if an email is to be assigned as spam or nonspam or diagnosis of a specific patient by certain disease based on known features of the patient like gender, the symptoms that he has and blood pressure, in another word, can be said that classification is a symbol of pattern recognition [7].

Classification is the process of training the objective function f in which each attribute x is a map to class label y that is already known. Resulting in a group of records which is the training set (training set), I every and each record includes a collection of attributes, in which the class is among one of them [8].

The model classification can be used for the following.

I. Descriptive modeling: the model of classification can work as a caption tool to show the difference between different classes with the same objects.

II. Predictive modeling: in this type of classification model, a label of the class that belongs to unknown data can be predicted [8], as shown in **Figure 1**.

The methods used in classification can be split into two categories as parametric and nonparametric problems. As a matter of fact, the basis of the parametric method is on the assumptions that the population normally distributed and the parameters are assessed to solve the problem [9]. On the other hand, there are no assumptions made about the distributions in the nonparametric methods and hence the distribution is free [10].

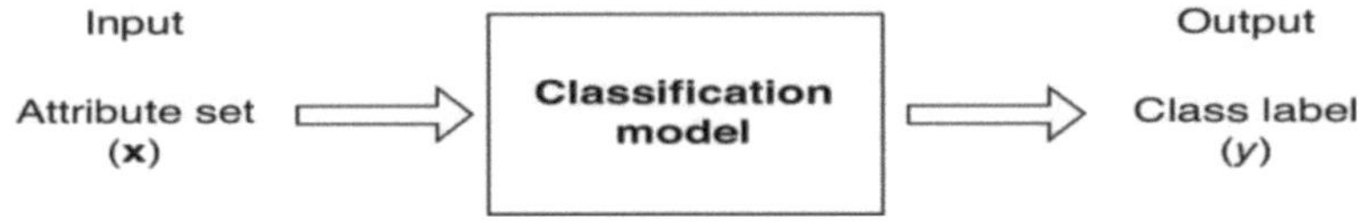

Figure 1.
Process of training the objective function f in which each attribute x is mapped.

3. Classification techniques

The classification techniques are as follows.

3.1 Decision tree

The decision is supported by using a tool like a decision tree by using the graph as a tree or modeling a variety of decisions and their potential effects, which include

DOI: http://dx.doi.org/10.5772/intechopen.85801

several examples of the outcomes of a chance event, costs of the resource, and utility [11].

Decision trees are usually used in the research of operations, more specific in analysis of the decision, to assist in the identification of the most of the strategies used to reach a goal, but they are a very popular tool to use in machine learning [11].

The induction of the decision tree is to learn the decision trees from the row of training in the class that is already labeled. A decision tree as can be considered as a flowchart, for instance, tree structure, in which the internal node stands for test on an attribute, and the outcome of this test is represented by the node of the leaf containing a class label [12].

3.2 K-star algorithm

An instance-based classifier called K-star or K*, is a class of the instance in the test step depending on the similar instance in the training step, as found by the function of the similarity. The difference between this algorithm and other instance-based learners is that this one uses a distance based on the entropy function. Classification based on the instance-based learners is made by comparing the instance to database examples that are previously classified. The basic assumption is that instances with similar classifications will be similar too. "Similar instance" and "similar classification" can be defined as follows: the instance-based components are the distance function that identifies the similarity between the two instances, and the classification function assigns how the instance similarities yield a final classification to classify the new instance. The entropic measure is used in K-star algorithm, depending on the likelihood of an instance transforming randomly into another by selecting among all potential transformations. The distance of the instance by using entropy as a meter is very helpful and the distance between the instances is measured with the help of the information theory. The distance between the instances is actually represented by the transformation complexity of one instance into another. It is being accomplished into two parts: first, a limited group of transformations is identified, which will assign one instance into another. Later, one instance (a) is tranformed to another instance (b) with the help of programs in a limited transformations sequence, beginning at (a) and ending at (b). A collection of points that is unbounded is given and a group of transformations that previously defined T is defined; group T has the value of. This t will be assigned as t: I → I. To assign instances with it, σ is used in the T (σ(a) = a). σ ending P, the group of all codes of the prefix from T*. Transformation on I is identified by members of T* and of P uniquely.

For the employment of the classifier for the instance-based of a that employs the distance measure of entropy, there is the necessity of a method to select values for the $x0$ parameters for attributes that are real and s for the attributes that are symbolic, as method employment the values returned by the measure of distance to give a prediction.

For every dimension, the selection of values must be made to the $x0$ parameters (for attributes that are real) and s (for attributes that are symbolic). The distance measure attitude as changes in these parameters is interesting. Function P* that considers the efficient number instances can be calculated using the expression[13]:

$$n0 \leq (\sum_{b} p * \frac{\frac{b}{a}}{\Sigma_b p * (\frac{b}{a})^{\wedge}2)} \leq N \text{ ....}$$

where N is considered to be the whole number of instances in the training and the instance number is in the training with the distance that considers the smallest from *an* (in this attribute).

Value for $x0$ (or so) is being selected by the K* algorithm, $n0$, and N with a number in between is selected and overturn the above expression. The nearest neighbor algorithm will be obtained by choosing $n0$ and weighted instances by choosing N. For convenience, the blending parameter "b" is used to specify the number in which the blending is different for $n0$, b = 0% and for N, b = 100%, with values of intermediate and linearly interpolated [13].

3.3 Neural network

The neural network is an analogous, information that considers distributed processing structure being composed of a processing element (which can have a local memory and implement operations that are considered as localized information processing) interrelated together as connections by using unidirectional signal channels. Each output is rlated to one element that connects with branches ("fans out") into many collaterals as like (everyone has the same signal which is the output signal of the processing element) [14].

3.4 Support vector machine

In COLT-92 by Boser, Guyon and Vapnik introduced support vector machine (SVM). Since that time, it has become popular. This algorithm was theoretically developed from the theory of the statistical learning, and it considers the well-motivated algorithm since the 1960s [15].

Pattern classification consider the main problem that deals with, that means different types of patterns is classified using this algorithm. Now, different sort of pattern exists, i.e., linear and nonlinear. Patterns that are linear can be distinguished easily or are able to be separated in low dimension easily, and on the other hand, the patterns that are nonlinear cannot be distinguish easily or are not able to be separated easily, and thus these patterns sorts require manipulation in order to be easily separated [15].

The SVM main idea is the formation of a hyperplane that is considered an optimal, that is, able to be used for classification, in order to split the linear patterns. The selection of the optimal hyperplane is based on the selection of a hyperplane among the group of hyperplanes for the classification of the patterns in which the hyperplane margin is maximized like the distance between the nearest point of each pattern and the hyperplane. The main goal of SVM is that the margin is maximized in order and the process of the classification is preformed correctly of the given patterns, i.e., when the margin size is larger, the classification of the patterns is more accurate [15, 18]. The hyperplane equation:

$$\text{Hyper plane, } aX + bY = C \ldots\ldots\ldots\ldots\ldots\ldots\ldots$$

The pattern that is given by using kernel functions is able to be assigned to higher space of dimension; the function of the kernel is $\Phi(x)$. I.e. x Φ (x), the various functions of kernel election are very necessary for the classification using SVM; usually, the functions of the kernel that are used contain RBF, linear sigmoid, and Poly. For example [14].

The Poly Kernel function equation is given as [14]:

$$K(x, y) = \langle x, y \rangle \hat{}\, p \ldots\ldots\ldots\ldots\ldots\ldots\ldots$$

The basic concept of support vector machine is that a group of training sample is given (a) that contains a distributed sample which is considered identical and independent; the sample has xi, in which xi belongs to the Rd, and yi belongs to the

$\{-1,1\}$ and they both as $\{(xi,yi)\}N$ i = 1, and they both refer to the classification input and output. The object is to determine wT.x + b = 0 that consider a hyperplane equation, in which two various samples are being split accurately. Hence, problem-solving with the classification that considers optimal is translated into quadratic programming for problems-solving. The search for a partition hyperplane is to maximize the area of bilateral blank (2/||w||), which means the weight of the margin has to be maximized. It is expressed as [14]:

$$\text{Min } \Phi(w) = \tfrac{1}{2} \| w \| 2 = \tfrac{1}{2} (w, w) \ldots\ldots\ldots\ldots\ldots\ldots$$

4. Case study

The main problem with the construction industry that contains a number of risks, and in order to minimize these risks, a model should be used to analyze these risks. A scientific research methodology is adopted which includes three stages:

4.1 Theoretical study

1. A review of the scientific literature and sources (books, magazines, engineering, research), which dealt with all of them.

2. Risk responses concept and strategies in construction projects.

3. Studying cost elements, types, and factors affecting it with the study of the causes of their appearance.

    a. Studying the artificial intelligence techniques and the steps of its procedures and its uses in the construction projects.

    b. Studying the simulation methods and the steps of its procedures and its uses in the construction projects.

4.2 Field study

The field study includes the following:

4.2.1 Open questionnaire

This stage includes conducting many interviews with experts. The interviews include managers and university professors, and other parts of the projects in the following ministries: the Ministry of Higher Education and Scientific Research, the Ministry of Construction and Housing, and the Ministry of Education. These interviews have a very important role in helping the researcher in the later stage, also discussion about the questionnaire which is initially prepared from the literature and previous studies as well as doing some modifications on the form and adding another questions with the help of the experts to make sure of the success of the method and questions presented.

4.2.2 Closed questionnaire

After the interviews with many experts have been finished. The problems of the research were divided into several groups which including the risks that cause to cost overruns, the top risk and their impacts on the projects, the strategies that are used for each risk, the reasons for risk response failure and finally the risks generated from risk response.

4.3 Stage of system building and software design

In the light of the responses received from the questionnaire, the practical study is as follows:

1. Planning of risk.
2. Identification of risk.
3. Analysis of risk using decision tree and K-star machine.
4. Risk response evaluation using neural network and support vector.

In this model, two types of classification were used, descriptive classification by using decision tree and predictive classification by using K-star and as follow:

- Identify the dependent variable.
- Identify the independent variable.
- Implement descriptive classification using a decision tree.
- Implement predictive classification using K-star.

4.4 Identify the independent variable of descriptive classification

The decision tree application is an example of a descriptive classification. This type of classification considers a number of attributes (variable) which affect the variable to be described. This type of classification is important to the variables that have an effect on the target.

This research describes the method of classification by using a decision tree to describe the qualitative analysis of the risks of project cost based on historical data. The data used to develop the classification model were the past data from various engineering works in different ministries. The method that is used to collect data is the direct data gathering from the engineering and the direct interview with the engineers and managers.

Results gained were collected from two parts: first one is the literature survey and the second one is the field of investigation (interview and questionnaire analysis) as mentioned before; 23 variables were considered as the independent variables; these variables are risks and their probabilities are considered too high, high, medium, low, and too low, and the impacts as too high, high, medium, low, too low, which are shown in **Table 1**.

4.5 Dependent variables

Qualitative analysis is considered to be the dependent variable which is too high, high, medium, low, too low, and each individual engineer or manager is used as the basic unit of the observation. Therefore this model is considered to be an attempt to make a model consisting of the independent variables which could describe the qualitative analysis classification.

RISKS
1-Price fluctuation
2-Inflation
3-Unavailability of information
4-Increase in cost due environment constrain
5-Financial difficulty by the contractor
6-financial difficulty by owner
7-Absence of measurement before advance
8-Design team performance
9-Inadequate owner requirement
10-Delay in agreement of design
11-Mismanagement of contract
12-Ambiguity of contract
13-Selection of team management
14-Miss selection of sit
15-Labor production
16-Luck of labor
17-Delay in deliver in equipment
18-Quality control on material
19-Exceptional circumstances and risks
20-Weather
21-Wrong estimation
22-Delay in the completing of the project
23-Increase in the cost of material and equipment

Table 1.
The identified risks.

4.6 Weka implementation: two techniques were used in this program

4.6.1 Decision tree implementation: Weka program

Waikato Environment for Knowledge Analysis (Weka) is a famous software in machine learning suite; the language used is Java; and University of Waikato, New Zealand developed this program. It is a software that considered as free, and the license of this program is a GNU General Public License. The Weka (said to rhyme similar to Mecca) is considered to be a workbench [16] which includes a group of tools for visualization and algorithms that are used to analyze the data and molding for the predictions; it is easy to access this function by using graphical user interface [15] and the version of Weka 3 that was developed in the early 1997 was used for many different implementation areas, especially for the purpose of education and research.

Several standard data mining tasks are supported by Weka, to be more specific, preprocessing of the data, regression, classification, clustering, visualization, and selection of the feature [17, 19], as shown in **Figure 2**.

The Explorer is in the GUI which is opened and the explorer is pressed on to insert the file that needs to be classified and by pressing the bottom open file to insert the file in the preprocess window which is used to choose and modify the data being acted on. As shown in **Figure 3**.

At this stage, the model was uploaded and full information such as relation means the name of the file, the total number of instances, attributes, type, the missing value, and others is shown in the figure above.

After this stage, a classifier was selected to perform the descriptive analysis as shown in **Figure 4**.

In the section of Classify at the top, there is a Classifier box. This box has a number of text area that provides the name of the classifier that the research work with, and by clicking on the tree bottom, there are several algorithms available under this option, the researcher selects j48 algorithm which one the application and implementations of C4.5 as shown in **Figure 5**.

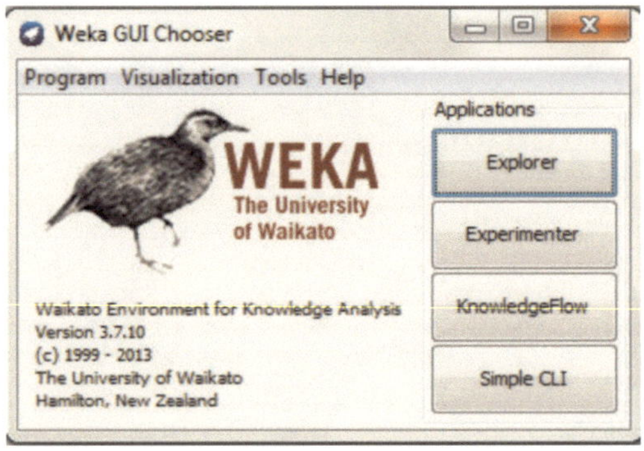

Figure 2.
Graphing component of WEKA 3.7.10 program.

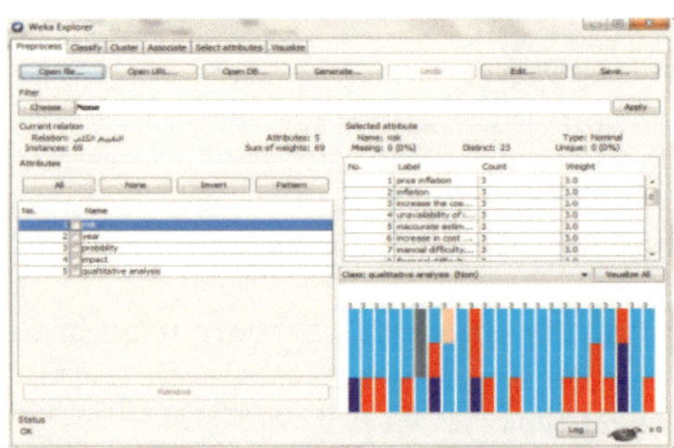

Figure 3.
Displays the preprocess window in the explorer.

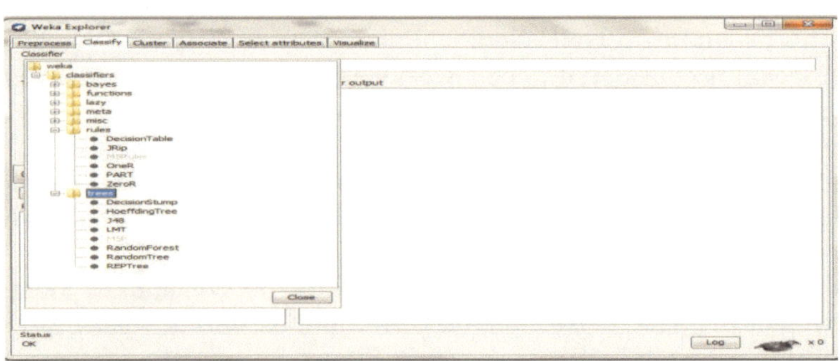

Figure 4.
Displays the process of selecting the classifier.

In this step, the properties of the algorithm are selected. In this model after the trial and error, the confidence factor is 0.25, the debug is false, min NUM obj is 2, NUM Folds are 3, and the unpruned option is true, which give the researcher the best results achieved as shown in **Tables 2** and **3**.

According to the tree, the risk with medium impact has the following probability: medium—13 risks, low—3 risks, and too low and high—there is no medium classification; while the risk with low impact has the following probability: medium there are 7 class low, too low has 1 class, low has 36 class, and high does not have

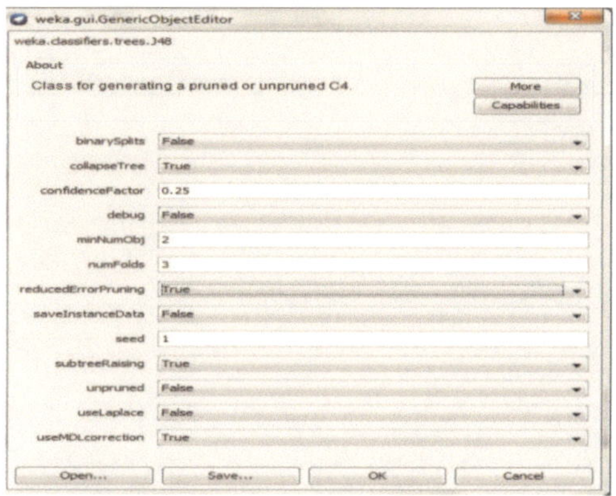

Figure 5.
Displays the process of selecting j48 properties.

Tp rate	Fp rate	Precision	Recall	F-measure	MCC	ROC area	Prc area	Class	Description of the results
1.000	0.031	0.714	1.000	0.833	0.832	0.970	0.638	High	The results show that this class is classified correctly as the Tp is 1 and Fp low and precision acceptable and the recall high, the MCC takes the classification between each two class and Roc area is high which indicates good performance for the high class and Prc is the medium indicator of the model performance
0.867	0.000	1.000	0.867	0.929	0.983	0.983	0.957	Medium	The results show that this class is classified kind off correctly as the Tp is 0.867 and Fp is zero and precision acceptable and the recall high, the MCC takes the classification between each two class and Roc area is high which indicate good performance for the medium class and

Tp rate	Fp rate	Precision	Recall	F-measure	MCC	ROC area	Prc area	Class	Description of the results
									Prc is the good indicator of the model performance consider very good
1.000	0.130	0.939	1.000	0.968	0.904	0.978	0.979	Low	The results show that this class is classified correctly as the Tp is 1 and Fp is low and precision high and the recall high, the MCC takes the classification between each two class and Roc area is high which indicates good performance for the low class and Prc is the good indicator of the model performance which considers very good
0.000	0.000	0.000	0.000	0.000	0.000	0.739	0.264	Too low	The results show that this class is classified incorrectly as the Tp is zero and Fp is zero and precision, the recall, the MCC are zero while Roc area is very low which indicates bad performance for the too low class and Prc is the good indicator of the model performance which considers very bad
0.000	0.000	0.000	0.000	0.000	0.000	0.493	0.014	Too high	The results show that this class is classified incorrectly as the Tp is zero and Fp is zero and precision, the recall, the MCC are zero while Roc area is very low which indicates bad performance for the too high class and Prc is the good indicator of the model performance which considers very bad
0.928	0.089	0.895	0.928	0.908	0.861	0.965	0.915		As a total cumulative result, its consider being good classification

Table 2.
The decision tree results in the WEKA program.

Risks	Actual	Classified
Price fluctuation	High	High
Inflation	Medium	Medium
Increase the cost of skilled labor	Medium	Medium
Unavailability of information	Low	Low
Inaccurate estimation	Low	Low
The increase in cost due environment	Too low	Low
Financial difficulty by the contractor	Low	Low
Financial difficulty by owner	Low	Low
The absence of measurement before	Low	Low
Delay in time of the project	High	High
Design team performance	Low	Low
Inadequate owner requirement	Low	Low
Delay in agreements of design	Low	Low
The ambiguity of contract	Low	Low
Miss selection of team management	Low	Low
Miss election of sit	Low	Low
Labor production	Medium	Medium
The decrease in labor	Medium	Medium
Delay in delivery in equipment	Medium	
Quality control on material	Low	Low
Unexpected condition	High	High
Weather	Low	Low
Mismanagement of the contract	Low	Low
Price fluctuation	Low	Low
Inflation	Low	Low
Increase the cost of skilled labor	Low	Low
Unavailability of information	Low	Low
Inaccurate estimation	Low	Low
The increase in cost due environment	Too low	Low
Financial difficulty by the contractor	Medium	Medium
Financial difficulty by owner	Low	Low
The absence of measurement before	Low	Low
Delay in time of the project	Medium	Medium
Design team performance	Medium	Medium
Inadequate owner requirement	Low	Low
Delay in agreements of design	Low	Low
The ambiguity of contract	Low	Low
Selection of team management	Low	Low
Miss election of sit	Low	Low
Labor production	Low	Low

Risks	Actual	Classified
The decrease in labor	Low	Low
Delay in delivery in equipment	Low	Low
Quality control on material	Medium	High
Unexpected condition	Medium	Medium
Weather	Low	Low
Mismanagement of the contract	Medium	Medium
Price fluctuation	Low	Low
Inflation	Low	Low
Increase the cost of skilled labor	Low	Low
Unavailability of information	Low	Low
Inaccurate estimation	Medium	Medium
The increase in cost due environment	Low	Low
Financial difficulty by the contractor	High	High
Financial difficulty by owner	Too high	Low
The absence of measurement before	Low	Low
Delay in time of the project	Medium	Medium
Design team performance	Low	Low
Inadequate owner requirement	Low	Low
Delay in agreements of design	Medium	Medium
The ambiguity of contract	Low	Low
Selection of team management	Low	Low
Miss election of sit	Low	Low
Labor production	Low	Low
The decrease in labor	Low	Low
Delay in delivery in equipment	Medium	High
Quality control on material	Low	Low
Unexpected condition	High	High
Weather	Low	Low
Mismanagement of the contract	Low	Low

Table 3.
The classified and the actual data of decision tree the WEKA program.

any class; on the other hand, the risk that has the impact high has class high with two of them are wrongly classified and the risks with impact too low and too high have the class of one too low and one too high, respectively, as shown in **Figure 6**.

4.6.2 K-star implementation: Weka program

As mentioned, Weka is a popular software for machine learning, and this type of algorithm will be used for predictive classification to predict the qualitative analysis of the risks for the periods 2014–2016 depending on the qualitative analysis for the previous periods from 2006 to 2014. The result is shown in **Table 4**.

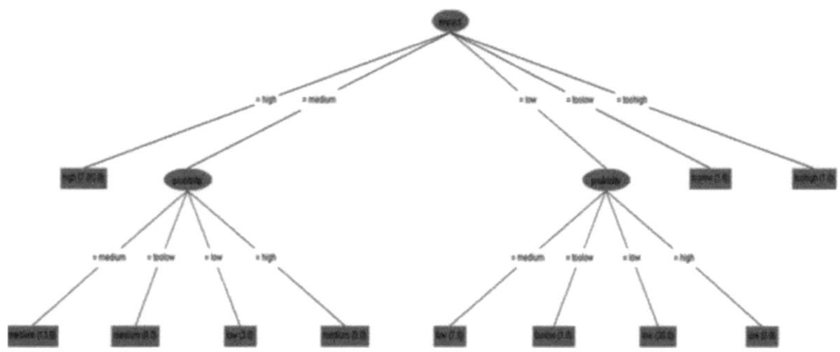

Figure 6.
Displays the tree of j48.

Risks	Actual	Classified
Price fluctuation	High	Medium
Inflation	Medium	Medium
Increase the cost of skilled labor	Medium	Medium
Unavailability of information	Low	Low
Inaccurate estimation	Low	Low
The increase in cost due environment	Too low	Low
Financial difficulty by the contractor	Low	Low
Financial difficulty by owner	Low	Low
The absence of measurement before	Low	Low
Delay in time of the project	High	High
Design team performance	Low	Low
Inadequate owner requirement	Low	Low
Delay in agreements of design	Low	Low
The ambiguity of contract	Low	Low
Miss selection of team management	Low	Low
Miss election of sit	Low	Low
Labor production	Medium	Medium
The decrease in labor	Medium	Medium
Delay in delivery in equipment	Medium	
Quality control on material	Low	Low
Unexpected condition	High	High
Weather	Low	Low
Mismanagement of the contract	Low	Low
Price fluctuation	Low	Low
Inflation	Low	Low
Increase the cost of skilled labor	Low	Low
Unavailability of information	Low	Low
Inaccurate estimation	Low	Low
The increase in cost due environment	Too low	Low
Financial difficulty by the contractor	Medium	Medium

Risks	Actual	Classified
Financial difficulty by owner	Low	Low
The absence of measurement before	Low	Low
Delay in time of the project	Medium	Medium
Design team performance	Medium	Medium
Inadequate owner requirement	Low	Low
Delay in agreements of design	Low	Low
The ambiguity of contract	Low	Low
Selection of team management	Low	Low
Miss election of sit	Low	Low
Labor production	Low	Low
The decrease in labor	Low	Low
Delay in delivery in equipment	Low	Low
Quality control on material	Medium	High
Unexpected condition	Medium	Medium
Weather	Low	Low
Mismanagement of the contract	Medium	Medium
Price fluctuation	Low	Low
Inflation	Low	Low
Increase the cost of skilled labor	Low	Low
Unavailability of information	Low	Low
Inaccurate estimation	Medium	Medium
The increase in cost due environment	Low	Low
Financial difficulty by the contractor	High	Medium
Financial difficulty by owner	Too high	Too low
The absence of measurement before	Low	Low
Delay in time of the project	Medium	Medium
Design team performance	Low	Low
Inadequate owner requirement	Low	Low
Delay in agreements of design	Medium	High
The ambiguity of contract	Low	Low
Selection of team management	Low	Low
Miss election of sit	Low	Low
Labor production	Low	Low
The decrease in labor	Low	Low
Delay in delivery in equipment	Medium	Medium
Quality control on material	Low	Low
Unexpected condition	High	Medium
Weather	Low	Low
Mismanagement of the contract	Low	Low

Table 4.
The classified and the actual data of K-star in the WEKA program.

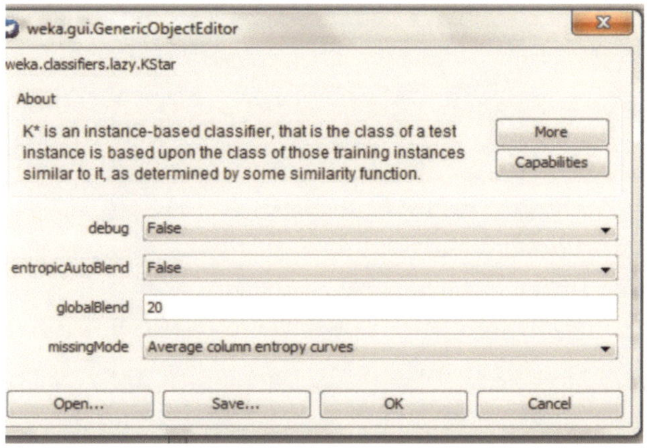

Figure 7.
Displays the process of selecting K-star properties.

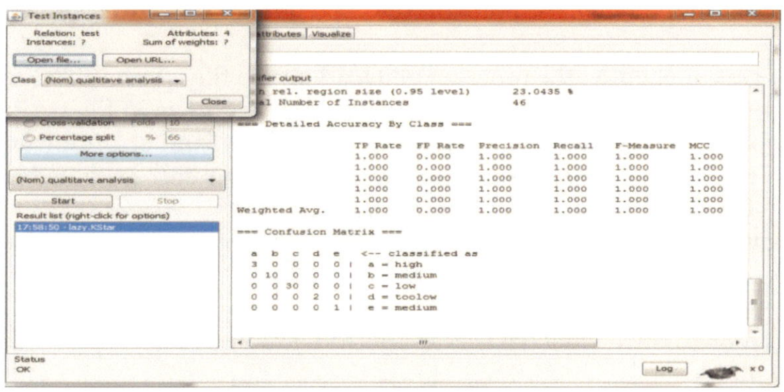

Figure 8.
Displays the process of uploading the test file.

Correctly classified instances	91.304%	This is considered being good classification accuracy
Incorrectly classified instances	8.6975	There is no classification error
Kappa statistic	81.85%	Consider being good value as compared to the realistic

Table 5.
The correctly and incorrectly classified instance using cross validation in K-star.

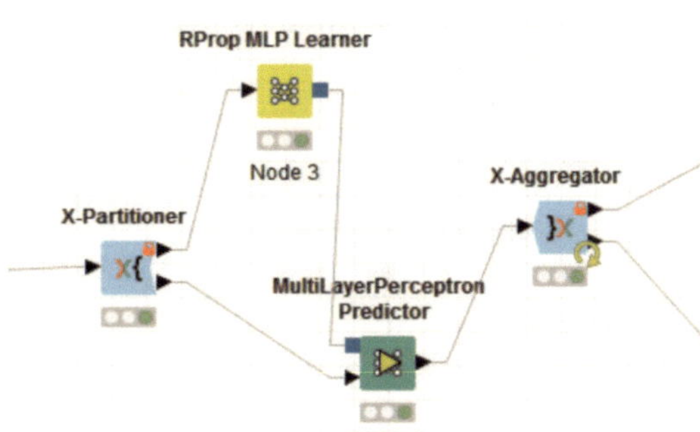

Figure 9.
Display neural network model.

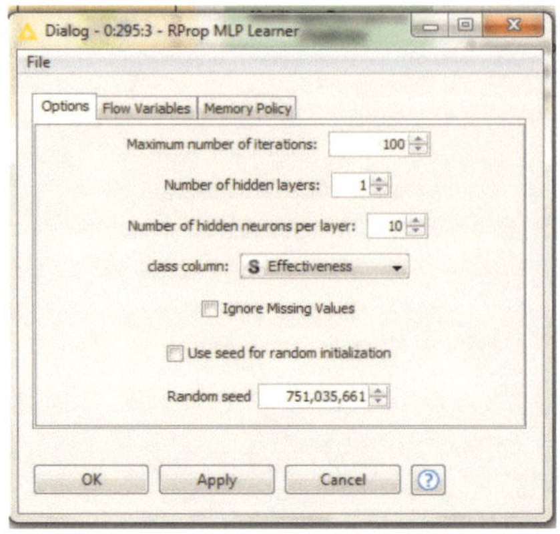

Figure 10.
Display configure menu.

Thus the probability for each instance is calculated in the category of the qualitative analysis, and the highest probability is taken for the classification of the new instance.

The process of opening the program and loading the file is mentioned earlier; the next step is choosing the properties of the algorithm as shown in **Figure** 7.

The global blending was taken as 20 after several trial and error; it was found to be the best result, the entropy autoblending which means entropy base blending in this case, it does not use for better accuracy.

The training data set has good accuracy, this high accuracy because the algorithm uses an entropy distance and use the whole data as training data. As shown in **Figure 8**.

After this step, the testing data set is uploading to perform the prediction classification.

In order to make a comparison between the two techniques, the whole data are used in cross-validation to make a comparison. As shown in **Table 5**.

4.6.3 KNIME implementation

Using the program, risk response failure in construction project was analyzed using the following techniques.

4.6.3.1 Neural network

This technique was used as part of the model to describe the risk response failure.

This workflow represents the neural network model right-click it and select "Configure" from the menu, as shown in **Figure 9**.

The max number of iterations was selected 100 and by trial and error the number of the hidden layers was 1 and hidden neuron were 10, as shown in **Figure 10**.

The results are shown in **Tables 6** and 7.

4.6.3.2 Support vector machine

This technique was used as part of the model to predict risk response failure. As shown in **Figures 11** and **12**.

DOI: http://dx.doi.org/10.5772/intechopen.85801

Project and year	Risks	Qualitative analyses	Risk response	Effectiveness	Effectiveness linguistic
1, 2006	Price fluctuation	Medium	Avoidance	3.33	Medium
1, 2006	Inflation	Medium	Avoidance	2.60	Low
1, 2006	Delay in completing of the project	High	Acceptance	3.07	Medium
1, 2006	Labor productivity	Medium	Acceptance	2.87	Medium
1, 2006	Exceptional circumstance and risks	High	Acceptance	1.85	Low
1, 2006	Wrong estimation	High	Avoidance	3.33	Medium
			Acceptance	2.51	Low
2, 2006	Price fluctuation	Medium	Avoidance	3.40	Medium
2, 2006	Delay in completing of the project	High	Acceptance	1.80	Low
2, 2006	Change in cost of equipment	Medium	Avoidance	2.87	Medium
2, 2006	Luck of the labor	Medium	Avoidance	2.90	Medium
2, 2006	Exceptional circumstance and risks	High	Acceptance	3.10	Medium
3, 2006	Delay in completing of the project	High	Avoidance	3.33	Medium
3, 2006	Labor productivity	Medium	Acceptance	3.13	Medium
3, 2006	Exceptional circumstance and risks	High	Acceptance	1.95	Low
3, 2006	Wrong estimation	High	Avoidance	2.67	Medium
4, 2006	Increase in the cost of skilled labor	Medium	Avoidance	3.07	Medium
4, 2006	Delay in completing of the project	High	Acceptance	2.60	Low
4, 2006	Change in cost of equipment	Medium	Avoidance	3.20	Medium
4, 2006	Luck of the labor	Medium	Avoidance	3	Medium
4, 2006	Exceptional circumstance and risks	High	Acceptance	2.80	Medium
5, 2006	Price fluctuation	Medium	Avoidance	3.20	Medium
5, 2006	Increase in the cost of skilled labor	Medium	Avoidance	2.60	Low
5, 2006	Delay in completing of the project	High	Acceptance	3.20	Medium
5, 2006	Luck of the labor	Medium	Avoidance	3.13	Medium
5, 2006	Exceptional circumstance and risks	High	Acceptance	1.85	Low
6, 2006	Delay in completing of the project	High	Acceptance	3.07	Medium
6, 2006	Change in cost of equipment	Medium	Avoidance	3.40	Medium
6, 2006	Luck of the labor	Medium	Avoidance	2.67	Medium

Project and year	Risks	Qualitative analyses	Risk response	Effectiveness	Effectiveness linguistic
6, 2006	Exceptional circumstance and risks	High	Acceptance	3.40	Medium
7, 2006	Price fluctuation	Medium	Avoidance	2.80	Medium
7, 2006	Increase in the cost of skilled labor	Medium	Acceptance	2.90	Medium
7, 2006	Delay in completing of the project	High	Acceptance	2.87	Medium
7, 2006	Luck of the labor	Medium	Avoidance	2.67	Medium
7, 2006	Exceptional circumstance and risks	High	Acceptance	2.60	Low
8, 2006	Price fluctuation	Medium	Avoidance	3.33	Medium
8, 2006	Increase in the cost of skilled labor	Medium	Avoidance	3.17	Medium
8, 2006	Delay in completing of the project	High	Acceptance	2.80	Medium
8, 2006	Luck of the labor	Medium	Avoidance	2.90	Medium
8, 2006	Exceptional circumstance and risks	High	Acceptance	1.90	Low
9, 2006	Increase in the cost of skilled labor	Medium	Avoidance	2.87	Medium
9, 2006	Delay in completing of the project	High	Acceptance	3.13	Medium
9, 2006	Change in cost of equipment	Medium	Avoidance	3.33	Medium
9, 2006	Luck of the labor	Medium	Avoidance	3.04	Medium
9, 2006	Exceptional circumstance and risks	High	Acceptance	3.40	Medium
10, 2006	Price fluctuation	Medium	Avoidance	2.67	Medium
10, 2006	Increase in the cost of skilled labor	Medium	Avoidance	2.77	Medium
10, 2006	Delay in completing of the project	High	Acceptance	3.27	Medium
10, 2006	Luck of the labor	Medium	Avoidance	3	Medium
10, 2006	Exceptional circumstance and risks	High	Acceptance	1.81	Low
11, 2006	Delay in completing of the project	High	Acceptance	3.3	Medium
11, 2006	Exceptional circumstance and risks	High	Acceptance	2.90	Medium
12, 2008	Finical difficulty by the contractor	Medium	Acceptance	3.13	Medium
12, 2008	Delay in completing of the project	Medium	Acceptance	2.67	Medium
12, 2008	Quality control of the material	Medium	Avoidance	3.17	Medium

Project and year	Risks	Qualitative analyses	Risk response	Effectiveness	Effectiveness linguistic
12, 2008	Mismanagement of the contract	Medium	Avoidance	2.90	Medium
12, 2008	Exceptional circumstance and risks	Medium	Acceptance	2.85	Medium
12, 2008	Wrong estimation	Medium	Acceptance	3.33	Medium
13, 2008	Finical difficulty by the contractor	Medium	Avoidance	2.60	Medium
13, 2008	Delay in completing of the project	Medium	Acceptance	2.04	Low
13, 2008	Quality control of the material	Medium	Acceptance	2.80	Medium
13, 2008	Exceptional circumstance and risks	Medium	Acceptance	2.90	Medium
14, 2008	Finical difficulty by the contractor	Medium	Avoidance	2.67	Medium
14, 2008	Quality control of the material	Medium	Avoidance	3.10	Medium
14, 2008	Wrong estimation	Medium	Acceptance	3.33	Medium
15, 2008	Finical difficulty by the contractor	Medium	Avoidance	3.13	Medium
15, 2008	Delay in completing of the project	Medium	Acceptance	2.95	Medium
15, 2008	Quality control of the material	Medium	Acceptance	1.81	Low
15, 2008	Exceptional circumstance and risks	Medium	Acceptance	3.07	Medium
16, 2008	Finical difficulty by the contractor	Medium	Medium	2.21	Low
16, 2008	Delay in completing of the project	Medium	Avoidance	3.20	Medium
16, 2008	Design team performance	Medium	Acceptance	3	Medium
16, 2008	Quality control of the material	Medium	Mitigate	2.90	Medium
16, 2008	Mismanagement of the contract	Medium	Acceptance	3.22	Medium
16, 2008	Exceptional circumstance and risks	Medium	Acceptance	2.67	Medium
16, 2008	Wrong estimation	Medium	Acceptance	3.23	Medium
17, 2008	Finical difficulty by the contractor	Medium	Avoidance	3.17	Medium
17, 2008	Delay in completing of the project	Medium	Acceptance	2.85	Medium
17, 2008	Design team performance	Medium	Mitigate	3.17	Medium

Project and year	Risks	Qualitative analyses	Risk response	Effectiveness	Effectiveness linguistic
17, 2008	Quality control of the material	Medium	Avoidance	2.22	Low
17, 2008	Exceptional circumstance and risks	Medium	Acceptance	2.67	Medium
17, 2008	Wrong estimation	Medium	Acceptance	1.81	Low
18, 2008	Finical difficulty by the contractor	Medium	Avoidance	2.90	Medium
18, 2008	Delay in completing of the project	Medium	Acceptance	2.80	Medium
18, 2008	Quality control of the material	Medium	Acceptance	2.87	Medium
18, 2008	Mismanagement of the contract	Medium	Avoidance	2.67	Medium
18, 2008	Wrong estimation	Medium	Acceptance	2.60	Medium
19, 2008	Finical difficulty by the contractor	Medium	Avoidance	3.33	Medium
19, 2008	Delay in completing of the project	Medium	Acceptance	2.67	Medium
19, 2008	Exceptional circumstance and risks	Medium	Acceptance	3.07	Medium
20, 2008	Finical difficulty by the contractor	Medium	Avoidance	2.33	Low
20, 2008	Delay in completing of the project	High	Acceptance	2.85	Medium
20, 2008	Exceptional circumstance and risks	Medium	Acceptance	3.03	Medium
20, 2008	Wrong estimation	Medium	Acceptance	2.80	Medium
21, 2008	Finical difficulty by the contractor	Medium	Avoidance	3.40	Medium
21, 2008	Delay in completing of the project	Medium	Acceptance	2.80	Medium
21, 2008	Quality control of the material	Medium	Avoidance	2.90	Medium
21, 2008	Mismanagement of the contract	Medium	Avoidance	2.67	Medium
21, 2008	Wrong estimation	Medium	Acceptance	3.13	Medium
22, 2008	Finical difficulty by the contractor	Medium	Avoidance	3.07	Medium
22, 2008	Delay in completing of the project	Medium	Acceptance	3.13	Medium
22, 2008	Design team performance	Medium	Mitigate	2.95	Medium
22, 2008	Quality control of the material	Medium	Avoidance	2.67	Medium
22, 2008	Exceptional circumstance and risks	Medium	Acceptance	3.07	Medium
22, 2008	Wrong estimation	Medium	Acceptance	3.40	Medium

Project and year	Risks	Qualitative analyses	Risk response	Effectiveness	Effectiveness linguistic
23, 2008	Finical difficulty by the contractor	Medium	Avoidance	3.21	Medium
23, 2008	Delay in completing of the project	Medium	Acceptance	2.07	Low
23, 2008	Design team performance	Medium	Acceptance	2.80	Medium
23, 2008	Quality control of the material	Medium	Avoidance	3.21	Medium
23, 2008	Exceptional circumstance and risks	Medium	Acceptance	2.67	Medium
23, 2008	Wrong estimation	Medium	Acceptance	3.20	Medium
24, 2008	Finical difficulty by the contractor	Medium	Avoidance	3.13	Medium
24, 2008	Delay in completing of the project	Medium	Acceptance	2.85	Medium
24, 2008	Quality control of the material	Medium	Avoidance	3.13	Medium
24, 2008	Exceptional circumstance and risks	Medium	Acceptance	3.40	Medium
24, 2008	Wrong estimation	Medium	Acceptance	2.67	Medium
25, 2008	Delay in completing of the project	Medium	Acceptance	3.07	Medium
25, 2008	Exceptional circumstance and risks	Medium	Acceptance	2.90	Medium
25, 2008	Wrong estimation	Medium	Acceptance	2.80	Medium
26, 2008	Delay in completing of the project	Medium	Acceptance	2.67	Medium
26, 2008	Design team performance	Medium	Acceptance	2.70	Low
26, 2008	Quality control of the material	Medium	Avoidance	2.55	Medium
26, 2008	Exceptional circumstance and risks	Medium	Acceptance	3.33	Medium
26, 2008	Wrong estimation	Medium	Acceptance	3.17	Medium
27, 2008	Finical difficulty by the contractor	Medium	Avoidance	2.80	Medium
27, 2008	Delay in completing of the project	Medium	Acceptance	3.40	Medium
27, 2008	Quality control of the material	Medium	Avoidance	3.17	Medium
27, 2008	Exceptional circumstance and risks	Medium	Acceptance	2.87	Medium
27, 2008	Wrong estimation	Medium	Acceptance	3.13	Medium
28, 2008	Delay in completing of the project	Medium	Acceptance	2.33	Low
28, 2008	Quality control of the material	Medium	Avoidance	3.04	Medium

Project and year	Risks	Qualitative analyses	Risk response	Effectiveness	Effectiveness linguistic
28, 2008	Exceptional circumstance and risks	Medium	Acceptance	3.21	Medium
28, 2008	Wrong estimation	High	Acceptance	2.73	Medium
29, 2008	Delay in completing of the project	Medium	Acceptance	2.77	Medium
29, 2008	Quality control of the material	Medium	Avoidance	3.27	Medium
29, 2008	Exceptional circumstance and risks	Medium	Acceptance	3.03	Medium
29, 2008	Wrong estimation	Medium	Acceptance	2.81	Medium
30, 2008	Delay in completing of the project	Medium	Acceptance	3.03	Medium
30, 2008	Quality control of the material	Medium	Avoidance	2.90	Medium
30, 2008	Exceptional circumstance and risks	Medium	Acceptance	3.33	Medium
30, 2008	Wrong estimation	Medium	Acceptance	2.33	Low
31, 2008	Delay in completing of the project	High	Acceptance	2.07	Low
31, 2008	Wrong estimation	Medium	Acceptance	2.87	Medium
32, 2008	Finical difficulty by the contractor	Medium	Avoidance	1.81	Low
32, 2008	Delay in completing of the project	High	Acceptance	3.33	Medium
32, 2008	Wrong estimation	Medium	Acceptance	2.60	Medium
33, 2014	Finical difficulty by the contractor	High	Avoidance	3.33	Medium
33, 2014	Finical difficulty by the owner	High	Avoidance	2.80	Medium
33, 2014	Delay in completing of the project	High	Avoidance	2.87	Medium
33, 2014	Change in cost of equipment	Medium	Acceptance	2.90	Medium
33, 2014	Exceptional circumstance and risks	High	Acceptance	2.10	Low
34, 2014	Wrong estimation	Medium	Avoidance	3.33	Medium
34, 2014	Finical difficulty by the contractor	Medium	Avoidance	2.13	Low
34, 2014	Finical difficulty by the owner	High	Acceptance	2.95	Medium
34, 2014	Delay in completing of the project	High	Avoidance	3.07	Medium
34, 2014	Change in cost of equipment	Medium	Acceptance	3.13	Medium
34, 2014	Exceptional circumstance and risks	High	Avoidance	2.60	Medium

Project and year	Risks	Qualitative analyses	Risk response	Effectiveness	Effectiveness linguistic
35, 2014	Finical difficulty by the contractor	Medium	Avoidance	2.20	Low
35, 2014	Finical difficulty by the owner	High	Acceptance	3	Medium
35, 2014	Delay in completing of the project	High	Avoidance	2.90	Medium
35, 2014	Change in cost of equipment	Medium	Acceptance	2.20	Low
35, 2014	Exceptional circumstance and risks	High	Avoidance	2.33	Low
36, 2014	Finical difficulty by the contractor	Medium	Avoidance	3.20	Medium
36, 2014	Finical difficulty by the owner	High	Acceptance	2.13	Low
36, 2014	Delay in completing of the project	High	Acceptance	2.85	Medium
36, 2014	Exceptional circumstance and risks	High	Acceptance	2.07	Low
37, 2014	Wrong estimation	Medium	Avoidance	2.61	Medium
37, 2014	Finical difficulty by the contractor	Medium	Avoidance	2.67	Medium
37, 2014	Finical difficulty by the owner	High	Acceptance	2.60	Medium
37, 2014	Delay in completing of the project	High	Acceptance	2.77	Medium
37, 2014	Exceptional circumstance and risks	High	Acceptance	2.80	Medium
38, 2014	Wrong estimation	Medium	Acceptance	1.87	Low
38, 2014	Finical difficulty by the contractor	Medium	Avoidance	2.67	Medium
38, 2014	Finical difficulty by the owner	High	Avoidance	2.60	Medium
38, 2014	Delay in completing of the project	High	Acceptance	3.13	Medium
38, 2014	Exceptional circumstance and risks	High	Acceptance	3.17	Medium
39, 2014	Finical difficulty by the contractor	High	Avoidance	2.90	Medium
39, 2014	Finical difficulty by the owner	High	Avoidance	2.80	Medium
39, 2014	Delay in completing of the project	High	Acceptance	2.90	Medium
39, 2014	Exceptional circumstance and risks	High	Acceptance	2.87	Medium
40, 2014	Finical difficulty by the owner	High	Avoidance	3.07	Medium
40, 2014	Delay in completing of the project	High	Acceptance	3.33	Medium

Project and year	Risks	Qualitative analyses	Risk response	Effectiveness	Effectiveness linguistic
40, 2014	Change in cost of equipment	Medium	Avoidance	2.04	Low
40, 2014	Exceptional circumstance and risks	High	Acceptance	3.40	Medium
41, 2014	Finical difficulty by the contractor	Medium	Avoidance	2.07	Low
41, 2014	Finical difficulty by the owner	High	Avoidance	2.77	Medium
41, 2014	Delay in completing of the project	Medium	Acceptance	2.27	Low
41, 2014	Exceptional circumstance and risks	High	Acceptance	3	Medium

Table 6.
The results of the risk response effectiveness in the 41 projects.

Risk response	Actual effectiveness	Predication effectiveness
Avoidance	Medium	Medium
Avoidance	Medium	Medium
Acceptance	Medium	Medium
Acceptance	Medium	Medium
Acceptance	Medium	Medium
Acceptance	Medium	Low
Avoidance	Low	Medium
Avoidance	Medium	Medium
Acceptance	Low	Medium
Avoidance	Medium	Medium
Avoidance	Medium	Medium
Acceptance	Medium	Medium
Acceptance	Medium	Medium
Acceptance	Medium	Medium
Acceptance	Medium	Medium
Acceptance	Medium	Medium
Avoidance	Medium	Low
Acceptance	Low	Medium
Avoidance	Medium	Medium
Avoidance	Medium	Medium
Acceptance	Medium	Medium
Avoidance	Low	Medium
Avoidance	Medium	Medium
Acceptance	Medium	Medium
Avoidance	Medium	Medium

Risk response	Actual effectiveness	Predication effectiveness
Acceptance	Medium	Medium
Acceptance	Medium	Medium
Avoidance	Medium	Medium
Avoidance	Medium	Medium
Acceptance	Medium	Medium
Avoidance	Medium	Medium
Avoidance	Medium	Medium
Acceptance	Medium	Medium
Avoidance	Low	Medium
Acceptance	Medium	Medium
Avoidance	Medium	Medium
Avoidance	Medium	Medium
Acceptance	Medium	Medium
Avoidance	Medium	Medium
Acceptance	Medium	Medium
Avoidance	Low	Medium
Acceptance	Medium	Medium
Avoidance	Medium	Medium
Avoidance	Medium	Medium
Acceptance	Medium	Medium
Avoidance	Low	Medium
Acceptance	Medium	Medium
Acceptance	Medium	Medium
Avoidance	Low	Medium
Acceptance	Medium	Medium
Acceptance	Medium	Medium
Acceptance	Medium	Medium
Acceptance	Medium	Medium
Acceptance	Medium	Medium
Avoidance	Medium	Medium
Avoidance	Medium	Medium
Acceptance	Medium	Medium
Acceptance	Medium	Medium
Acceptance	Low	Medium
Acceptance	Medium	Medium
Acceptance	Low	Low
Acceptance	Medium	Medium
Avoidance	Medium	Medium
Avoidance	Medium	Medium
Acceptance	Medium	Medium
Acceptance	Low	Medium

Risk response	Actual effectiveness	Predication effectiveness
Acceptance	Medium	Medium
Acceptance	Medium	Medium
Acceptance	Medium	Medium
Avoidance	Medium	Medium
Acceptance	Medium	Medium
Mitigate	Medium	Medium
Acceptance	Medium	Medium
Avoidance	Medium	Medium
Acceptance	Low	Medium
Acceptance	Low	Medium
Acceptance	Medium	Medium
Acceptance	Low	Medium
Mitigate	Medium	Medium
Avoidance	Low	Medium
Acceptance	Medium	Medium
Acceptance	Medium	Medium
Avoidance	Medium	Medium
Acceptance	Medium	Medium
Avoidance	Medium	Low
Acceptance	Medium	Medium
Acceptance	Medium	Medium
Avoidance	Medium	Medium
Acceptance	Medium	Medium
Acceptance	Medium	Medium
Avoidance	Medium	Medium
Acceptance	Medium	Low
Acceptance	Medium	Low
Avoidance	Medium	Medium
Acceptance	Medium	Low
Mitigate	Medium	Medium
Avoidance	Medium	Medium
Acceptance	Medium	Medium
Acceptance	Low	Medium
Avoidance	Medium	Medium
Acceptance	Medium	Medium
Avoidance	Medium	Low
Acceptance	Low	Medium
Acceptance	Medium	Medium
Acceptance	Medium	Medium
Acceptance	Medium	Medium
Acceptance	Medium	Medium

Risk response	Actual effectiveness	Predication effectiveness
Acceptance	Low	Medium
Mitigate	Medium	Medium
Avoidance	Medium	Medium
Acceptance	Medium	Medium
Avoidance	Medium	Medium
Acceptance	Medium	Medium
Acceptance	Medium	Medium
Avoidance	Medium	Medium
Acceptance	Medium	Medium
Acceptance	Medium	Medium
Acceptance	Low	Medium
Acceptance	Low	Medium
Acceptance	Medium	Medium
Acceptance	Medium	Medium
Acceptance	Medium	Medium
Avoidance	Medium	Medium
Acceptance	Medium	Medium
Acceptance	Medium	Medium
Acceptance	Medium	Medium
Avoidance	Low	Medium
Acceptance	Medium	Medium
Acceptance	Medium	Medium
Acceptance	Medium	Medium
Acceptance	Medium	Medium
Acceptance	Medium	Medium
Avoidance	Medium	Medium
Acceptance	Medium	Medium
Acceptance	Medium	Medium
Acceptance	Medium	Medium
Acceptance	Medium	Medium
Acceptance	Medium	Medium
Avoidance	Low	Medium
Acceptance	Medium	Medium
Acceptance	Medium	Medium
Avoidance	Medium	Low
Acceptance	Medium	Low
Avoidance	Medium	Low
Avoidance	Low	Low
Acceptance	Medium	Medium

Table 7.
Show the actual effectiveness and the predication effectiveness of risk response using neural network results.

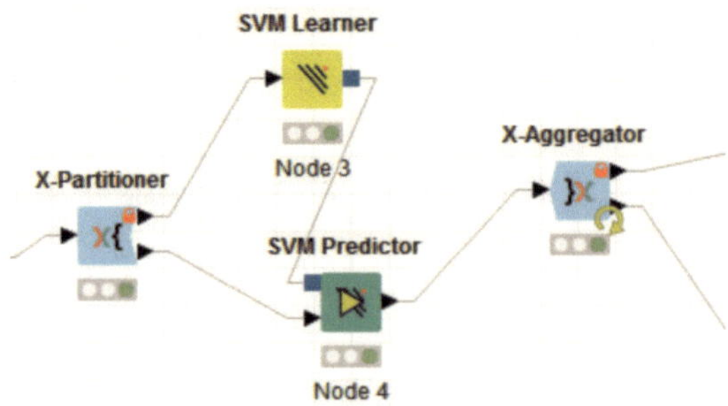

Figure 11.
Display support vector machine model.

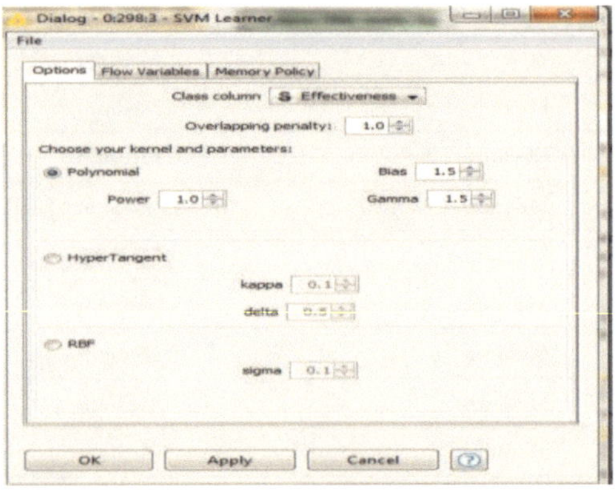

Figure 12.
Display support vector machine learner menu.

Class	True post	False post	True neg	False neg	Recall	Precision	sensitivity	Specify	f-mean	Accuracy	Description
Medium	123	23	0	0	1	0.842	1	0.0	0.941		The results show data classified correctly and the result perform well
Low	0	0	123	23	0.0	0.0	0	1	0		The results show that this class is not classified correctly as there is a lot of error in the low class and the Precision, and also the f measure is less that indicate the reason to lower the classification accuracy
Overall										84.2	

Table 8.
Support vector machine results.

When clicking on the SVM learner node the following window appears. The results are shown in **Tables 8** and **9**.

Risk response	Actual effectiveness	Predication effectiveness
Avoidance	Medium	Medium
Avoidance	Medium	Medium
Acceptance	Medium	Medium
Acceptance	Medium	Medium
Acceptance	Medium	Medium
Acceptance	Medium	Medium
Avoidance	Low	Medium
Avoidance	Medium	Medium
Acceptance	Low	Medium
Avoidance	Medium	Medium
Avoidance	Medium	Medium
Acceptance	Medium	Medium
Acceptance	Medium	Medium
Acceptance	Medium	Medium
Acceptance	Medium	Medium
Acceptance	Medium	Medium
Avoidance	Medium	Medium
Acceptance	Low	Medium
Avoidance	Medium	Medium
Avoidance	Medium	Medium
Acceptance	Medium	Medium
Avoidance	Low	Medium
Avoidance	Medium	Medium
Acceptance	Medium	Medium
Avoidance	Medium	Medium
Acceptance	Medium	Medium
Acceptance	Medium	Medium
Avoidance	Medium	Medium
Avoidance	Medium	Medium
Acceptance	Medium	Medium
Avoidance	Medium	Medium
Avoidance	Medium	Medium
Acceptance	Medium	Medium
Avoidance	Low	Medium
Acceptance	Medium	Medium
Avoidance	Medium	Medium
Avoidance	Medium	Medium

Risk response	Actual effectiveness	Predication effectiveness
Acceptance	Medium	Medium
Avoidance	Medium	Medium
Acceptance	Medium	Medium
Avoidance	Low	Medium
Acceptance	Medium	Medium
Avoidance	Medium	Medium
Avoidance	Medium	Medium
Acceptance	Medium	Medium
Avoidance	Low	Medium
Acceptance	Medium	Medium
Acceptance	Medium	Medium
Avoidance	Low	Medium
Acceptance	Medium	Medium
Acceptance	Medium	Medium
Acceptance	Medium	Medium
Acceptance	Medium	Medium
Acceptance	Medium	Medium
Avoidance	Medium	Medium
Avoidance	Medium	Medium
Acceptance	Medium	Medium
Acceptance	Medium	Medium
Acceptance	Low	Medium
Acceptance	Medium	Medium
Acceptance	Low	Medium
Acceptance	Medium	Medium
Avoidance	Medium	Medium
Avoidance	Medium	Medium
Acceptance	Medium	Medium
Acceptance	Low	Medium
Acceptance	Medium	Medium
Acceptance	Medium	Medium
Acceptance	Medium	Medium
Avoidance	Medium	Medium
Acceptance	Medium	Medium
Mitigate	Medium	Medium
Acceptance	Medium	Medium
Avoidance	Medium	Medium
Acceptance	Low	Medium
Acceptance	Low	Medium
Acceptance	Medium	Medium

Risk response	Actual effectiveness	Predication effectiveness
Acceptance	Low	Medium
Mitigate	Medium	Medium
Avoidance	Low	Medium
Acceptance	Medium	Medium
Acceptance	Medium	Medium
Avoidance	Medium	Medium
Acceptance	Medium	Medium
Avoidance	Medium	Medium
Acceptance	Medium	Medium
Acceptance	Medium	Medium
Avoidance	Medium	Medium
Acceptance	Medium	Medium
Acceptance	Medium	Medium
Avoidance	Medium	Medium
Acceptance	Medium	Medium
Acceptance	Medium	Medium
Avoidance	Medium	Medium
Acceptance	Medium	Medium
Mitigate	Medium	Medium
Avoidance	Medium	Medium
Acceptance	Medium	Medium
Acceptance	Low	Medium
Avoidance	Medium	Medium
Acceptance	Medium	Medium
Avoidance	Medium	Medium
Acceptance	Low	Medium
Acceptance	Medium	Medium
Acceptance	Medium	Medium
Acceptance	Medium	Medium
Acceptance	Medium	Medium
Acceptance	Low	Medium
Mitigate	Medium	Medium
Avoidance	Medium	Medium
Acceptance	Medium	Medium
Avoidance	Medium	Medium
Acceptance	Medium	Medium
Acceptance	Medium	Medium
Avoidance	Medium	Medium
Acceptance	Medium	Medium
Acceptance	Medium	Medium

Risk response	Actual effectiveness	Predication effectiveness
Acceptance	Low	Medium
Acceptance	Low	Medium
Acceptance	Medium	Medium
Acceptance	Medium	Medium
Acceptance	Medium	Medium
Avoidance	Medium	Medium
Acceptance	Medium	Medium
Acceptance	Medium	Medium
Acceptance	Medium	Medium
Avoidance	Low	Medium
Acceptance	Medium	Medium
Acceptance	Medium	Medium
Acceptance	Medium	Medium
Acceptance	Medium	Medium
Acceptance	Medium	Medium
Avoidance	Medium	Medium
Acceptance	Medium	Medium
Acceptance	Medium	Medium
Acceptance	Medium	Medium
Acceptance	Medium	Medium
Acceptance	Medium	Medium
Avoidance	Low	Medium
Acceptance	Medium	Medium
Acceptance	Medium	Medium
Avoidance	Medium	Medium
Acceptance	Medium	Medium
Avoidance	Medium	Medium
Avoidance	Low	Medium
Acceptance	Medium	Medium

Table 9.
Show the actual effectiveness and the predication effectiveness of risk response using support vector machine results.

5. Conclusions

1. The result from the statistical analysis results in a period of (2006–2007) show that the risks that have the highest qualitative analysis are the same that resulting from the classification result by using j48 algorithm

2. The result from the statistical analysis results in the period of (2014–2016) show that the risks that have the highest qualitative analysis are the same that resulting from the classification result by using j48 algorithm except for one

risk which is the quality control on the material and expertise in execution and that leads to an error.

3. The result from the statistical analysis results in the period of (2014–2016) show that the risks that have the highest qualitative analysis are same that resulting from the classification result by using j48 algorithm except for two risks which are financial difficulty by owner and Changes in the purchase costs or delay in the delivery of equipment and machinery and that leads to an error.

4. Different risks were found due to the different condition of these periods, however, some risks were the same as the delay in completing the project, exceptional circumstances, and the wrong estimation existed in every period

5. The decision tree is a successful quality technique in risk analysis

The result from the statistical analysis results in a period of 2014–2016 showed that the risks that have the highest qualitative analysis are same that resulting from the classification result by using K-star algorithm except for one risk which is financial difficulty by owner.

Second: Risk response identification

- In the periods of (2006–2007) the method that used for risk response selection was historical information for similar previous projects has the mean of 4.03 that means often this method used for selection.

- In the periods of (2008–2013) the method that used for risk response selection was historical information for similar previous projects has the mean of 3.73 that means often this method used for selection.

- In the periods of (2014–2016) the method that used for risk response selection was historical information for similar previous projects has the mean of 3.80 that mean often this method used for selection.

- The existing methods and tools for selecting a risk response are based on historical information for similar previous projects, m.aking them easily affected by anxiety, uncertainty.

- Three techniques to identify risk response failure.

    a. The decision tree shows the high accuracy and that because it considers the best algorithm in prediction of nominal class

    b. The neural network shows the lower accuracy as the nature of the algorithm tends more to the numerical class.

    c. The support vector machine show good results close to the decision tree

- The most important reasons that risk response fails in the period of (2006–2007) were The difficulty of implementing a risk-response plan correctly for internal factors (terrorism and sabotage), Multiple decision sources for selecting a response strategy, Inadequate strategy with high risk and The inability to introduce sophisticated management methods to respond to risks.

- The most important reasons that risk response fails in the period of (2008–2013) were Changes in the cost criteria that have been estimated at the planning stage of the project to the implementation stage, Inadequate strategy with high risk and The inability to introduce sophisticated management methods to respond to risks.
- The most important reasons that risk response fails in the period of (2014–2016) are negligence of supervisors in the follow-up to the risk response plan, lack of funds for training and continuous development of the risk response team, inadequate strategy with high risk, delay in the disbursement of financial dues by the responsible party, the difficulty of implementing a risk-response plan correctly for internal factors (terrorism and sabotage) and The inability to introduce sophisticated management methods to respond to risks.
- The period of (2014) shows many reasons that led to risk response failure in construction projects due to the condition of the country.

Author details

Hafeth I. Naji[1], Rouwaida Hussein Ali[2*] and Ehsan Ali Al-Zubaidi[3]

1 Civil Engineering Department, University of Diyala, Diayla, Iraq

2 Civil Engineering Department, University of Baghdad, Diayla, Iraq

3 Department of Computer and Internet, Faculty of Physical Planning, University of Kufa, Kufa, Iraq

*Address all correspondence to: rowedahhussien@gmail.com

References

[1] Ali BM. The reality of risk management and its importance in industrial organizations, field study in the spinning and weaving factory in Mosul [Master thesis]. Faculty of Management and Economics, University of Mosul; 2004

[2] Taylor I, Bassler J. Application of ANSI Standard to Space Station Resources. INOSE International Proceedings, IEEE. 1997;**83**(3):345-377

[3] Norris C, Perry J, Simon P. Project Risk Analysis and Management. The Association for Project Management; 2000

[4] Coppin B. Artificial Intelligence Illuminated. Jones & Bartlett Learning; 2004

[5] Nilsson NJ. Artificial Intelligence: A New Synthesis. New York: Morgan Kaufmann; 2002

[6] Martínez DM, Fernández-Rodríguez JC. Artificial Intelligence applied to project success: A literature review. International Journal of Interactive Multimedia & Artificial Intelligence. 2015;**3**(5)

[7] Alpaydin E. Introduction to Machine Learning. MIT Press; 2010. p. 9. ISBN: 978-0-262-01243-0

[8] Tan PN, Steinbach M, Kumar V. Introduction to Data Mining. Addison-Wesley Companion Book Site; 2006

[9] Zhang D, Huang H, Chen Q, Jiang Y. Comparison of credit scoring models. In: Third International Conference of Natural Computation; 2007

[10] Berry MJA, Linoff GS. Data Mining Techniques for Marketing, Sales and Customer Support. John Wiley & Sons, Inc; 1997

[11] Quinlan JR. Simplifying decision trees. International Journal of Man-Machine Studies. 1987;**27**(3):221

[12] Handaga B, Handaga B. A new classification technique based on hybrid fuzzy soft set theory and supervised fuzzy c-means [Doctoral dissertation]. Malaysia: Universiti Tun Hussein Onn; 2013

[13] Cleary JG, Trigg LE. K*: An instance-based learner using an entropic distance measure. In: 12th International Conference on Machine Learning. Morgan Kaufmann; 1995. pp. 108-114

[14] Archana S, Elangovan K. Survey of classification techniques in data mining. International Journal of Computer Science and Mobile Applications. 2014; **2**(2):65-71

[15] Holmes G, Donkin A, Witten IH. WEKA: A machine learning workbench (PDF). In: Proceedings of the Second Australia and New Zealand Conference on Intelligent Information Systems; Brisbane, Australia; 1994

[16] Witten IH, Frank E, Hall MA. Data Mining Practical Machine Learning Tools and Techniques. 3rd ed. USA: Elsevier; 2011

[17] Reutemann P, Pfahringer B, Frank E. Proper: A toolbox for learning from relational data with propositional and multi-instance learners. In: 17th Australian Joint Conference on Artificial Intelligence (AI2004). Springer-Verlag; 2004 [Retrieved: June 25, 2007]

[18] Pao YH. Neural net computing for pattern recognition. In: Handbook of Pattern Recognition and Computer Vision. 1993. pp. 125-162

[19] Aghila G. A survey of Naive Bayes machine learning approach in text document classification. 2010. arXiv preprint: arXiv-1003.1795